MW01536973

MY BEE-GINNING

Earl Schnell

Copyright © 2022 Earl Schnell
All rights reserved
First Edition

PAGE PUBLISHING, INC.
Conneaut Lake, PA

First originally published by Page Publishing 2022

ISBN 978-1-6624-6654-0 (pbk)
ISBN 978-1-6624-6655-7 (digital)

Printed in the United States of America

Contents

Introduction

I started beekeeping because I thought that it would be interesting. I could help save the bees while getting a source of really good honey. I purchased a large hive, which was very mean. I placed the hive a good distance from my house, yet the bees would come up and sting me. I tried to move them behind a building. I moved the hive, but the bees went back to the original location. I had an overwhelming mess. On my first year, I harvested five gallons of honey. This sounded good except I lost all my colonies that winter due to mites and starvation. I thought that I had made every rookie mistake possible. Little did I know that I had many more problems to come.

I started seeking information and help to learn and avoid any more mistakes. I joined several local bee clubs, researched the internet, and asked a lot of questions. Even after all my efforts, I simply did not understand how to take care of my bees. On my second year, I learned how to catch swarms, and I caught nineteen wild swarms. I sold a few of the swarms and again lost all the remaining colonies. This time, I lost my bees before winter. I didn't know that the stronger colonies would kill the smaller ones due to robbing or that the bees would leave due to improper use of mite treatments. I thought that I made every mistake possible in my first year only to find out I had many more mistakes to make. I continued attending four local bee clubs and still did not understand how to take care of my bees. Each club would explain how to do things in different ways. These clubs would have guest speakers who either were opinionated or would use so many technical terms that they were very hard for me to understand. I did not understand why things were done so that I would know what and when to do things.

I set out to understand the whole beekeeping cycle. I had a small beekeeping store. I soon realized that I could learn something from every beekeeper who came to my store. The more experienced beekeepers would tell me how they were successful with their bees, and the less experienced helped me to look for more answers. The more I learned, the more I wanted to know. I started a bee club after receiving several requests for a club in our town. I was now under pressure to ramp up my knowledge of beekeeping. I started out trying to make a beekeeping calendar. I had no idea that I would learn so much in a short time. I asked questions at several local bee clubs and posted questions on their websites, and I asked questions to as many experienced beekeepers as possible.

I then found a master beekeeper that placed me on the right path. He answered my many questions. He suggested some books that I should read. The books and answers that I received from the various sources contained big words and technical terms which were hard for me to understand as a newer beekeeper. I used the information and suggested resources as a learning tool. After much researching, reading, thinking, and asking questions, I felt a sense of accomplishment. I finally understood most of the beekeeping process for the first time. Now I was able to understand most everything that I had learned from the many sources. I knew what information was correct and which information was just opinions. I was able to fill in the many blanks in the beekeeping cycle because I understood the process. All I had to do now is to organize and break the information down so that a new beekeeper could easily understand. To do this, I enlisted the help of a member of our new club. It was my great fortune that this person was not only a beginner beekeeper but also an educator. Leslie Parker's contributions included suggesting, correcting, editing, and rearranging the material to make it easier for the beginner beekeeper to understand. I greatly appreciate her help.

In this book, I hope to help all new beekeepers avoid the mistakes that I made so that they would be successful in their very first year and beyond. There would always be something to learn. I wanted to find a standard way for the beginner beekeeper to be able to be successful in their first year. While there wasn't really a standard way to take care of bees, there were proven methods to use to be successful in the first year. Every attempt has been made to make the information about beekeeping in this book as accurate as possible.

Now about you. So you want to be a beekeeper? Bees are fascinating. The more you learn about them, the more you will want to learn. Beekeeping can be a real challenge if you don't know how to do things from the start. Take the time and effort to know the basics. On the other hand, beekeeping can be fun and exciting, not to mention the honey. The single biggest problem that the new beekeeper has is not knowing how to check for mites and how to treat for mites. Make sure that you learn how to control mites before getting your bees. This is very important, and I almost guarantee that your bees will die if you don't.

Before getting your bees, it is important that you understand the causes for your bees to die or leave your hive (abscond). Planning in the beginning will help you succeed in your first year. Winter or early spring is the main time when bee colonies die. This is due to starvation or being weakened by mites. Spring and summer losses are mainly due to queen loss. Beekeepers accidently kill their queen, or a virgin queen may not be able to return after mating. Robbing and beetles along with improper mite treatments can lead to colony loss. Wax moths can take over a weak colony. These invading pests and diseases seem to be the cause of colony loss. However, colony loss is usually the result of a colony weakened by mites or improper care. Planning and hive inspections can take care of most issues before they result in colony loss.

Safety should always be the most important consideration with any hobby. Beekeeping is no exception. The biggest safety hazards that a beekeeper is being exposed to the various mite treatments. Oxalic acid and formic acid are commonly used to treat mites. There are other types of chemical mite treatments as well. Oxalic acid is either vaporized or combined with other ingredients and placed into the hive. Formic acid is placed in the hive on manufacture-supplied material. Oxalic acid vapors can cause damage to your eyes, nose, and lungs. The liquid form can cause burns. Formic acid has similar health issues. Therefore the proper safety equipment must always be used when using any type of mite treatments. It is very important for the bees and for the beekeeper to always follow the manufacturer's instructions.

Wax moth

The Bees

• •

There are many species of honeybees. Some include Italian, Russian, Carniolan, Cordovan, and more. The new beekeeper may want to purchase the bees with the least defensive behavior as possible. These normally are the Italian, Carniolan, or a mixture. Honeybees aren't aggressive, but they can be very defensive. The bees are only trying to protect their young and their food stores. The Russian bees are one of the most defensive. New beekeepers may want to avoid Russian bees, while more experienced beekeepers may want them for their ability to survive adverse conditions. There are beekeepers who wear shorts when working with their bees, and then on the other extreme, there are beekeepers who have to wear a full suit just to open the hive. A new beekeeper will need to develop a comfort level around bees. Experienced beekeepers know the importance of being gentle with their bees and to always use a smoker. The calmer the bees, the easier it will be for the beekeeper. The less defensive bees will make this much easier.

In the following paragraphs, the different types of bees in a hive will be explained. The length of time for bee development is different depending if the egg laid is going to be a worker, a drone, or a queen. Understanding this time difference will help plan when to do certain beekeeping task like to prevent swarming or when to make splits.

The queen

The queen is a mature female. She has the longest life span in the colony living for up to three years. A good queen may lay 1,500–2,000 eggs in a single day. She can lay over 200,000 eggs during her lifetime, while mating with multiple drones on her original mating flight. The queen determines the sex of the egg being laid. The worker bees build the comb with different-size cells. The queen will lay an unfertilized egg in the bigger comb cells and a fertilized egg in the normal-size comb cells. Fertilized eggs will become female worker bees, and unfertilized eggs will become male bees called drones. The males are bigger than the female worker bees, therefore requiring a bigger cell. The queen will be very prolific egg layer in her first year and will slow as she gets older.

Queen

The queen is larger than the other bees in the hive and has a slim torpedo shape. She does have a stinger but only uses it to kill other queens. It takes sixteen days from egg to hatching to make a queen. Under normal conditions, a hive will have only one queen.

Queen cell

The queen's pheromone causes the bees to work together to accomplish the needed tasks. A young queen emits a strong pheromone, and as she gets older, the strength of her pheromone starts to subside. This is why a hive with a younger queen is less likely to swarm. The queen is thought to be in charge, but it is really the worker bees who are really in charge. The worker bees give the queen more or less food, which regulates when and how many eggs the queen will lay. The queen is expected to lay many eggs per day. The workers will replace the queen if she slows down for any reason or if her pheromones are too low. The workers will form queen cells either in the middle of the foundation or at the bottom of the frame. If the queen cells are in the middle of the foundation, the workers are going to replace the queen, and if the queen cells are on the bottom of the frame, the bees are going to swarm. Every colony must have a queen. A hive without a queen will become much smaller and eventually abscond.

The worker bee

Worker

Workers carrying pollen into the hive.

The Worker Bee Lifecycle

THE WORKER BEE

Day 1 Egg	1 Unsealed
Day 2	2
Day 3	3
Day 4 Larvae	1
Day 5	2
Day 6	3
Day 7	4
Day 8	5
Day 9	6
Day 10 Pupa	1 Sealed Brood
Day 11	2
Day 12	3
Day 13	4
Day 14	5
Day 15	6
Day 16	7
Day 17	8
Day 18	9
Day 19	10
Day 20	11
Day 21 Emerge	12 Worker Bee
Day 1 Bee	1 Clean out cells
Day 2	2
Day 3	3
Day 4	1 Feed older larvae
Day 5	2
Day 6	3
Day 7	1 Feed young larvae and queen
Day 8	2
Day 9	3
Day 10	4
Day 11	5
Day 12	6
Day 13	7
Day 14	1 Wax secretion
Day 15	2
Day 16	3
Day 17	4
Day 18	5
Day 19	1 Hive cleaning, gaurding the hive, ventilation the hive.
Day 20	2
Day 21	3
Day 1 as Forager	1 Collect necrar, water, pollen and propolis
Day 2	2
Day 3	3
Day 4	4
Day 5	5
Day 6	6
Day 7	7
Day 8	8
Day 9	9
Day 10	10
Day 11	11
Day 12	12
Day 13	13
Day 14	14
Day 15	15
Day 16	16
Day 17	17
Day 18	18
Day 19	19
Day 20	20
Day 21	21

Wax secretion comb building, pollen and nectar storage. A large number of the wax building bees exit the hive when the bees swarm. It will be their job to quickly build wax comb in the swarm's new hve.

Adult bees will become foragers until their death. Around 15 days as a forager. Foragers usually die when their wings are worn out and they can no longer fly. Winter bees live longer due to not having to fly. This timing is very important when planning your beekeeping tasks.

Guard Bees

Worker bees are sexually underdeveloped females. There can be as many as 60,000 workers in a single colony. They are called workers because that is what they do. They collect food and water for the colony, build wax comb, do the housework, maintain the interior temperatures of the hive, guard the hive against intruders, and forage for nectar, pollen, and water in the later stage of their life. The worker bees give their life protecting the hive. The worker can only sting once because their stinger and venom sac are ripped out of them when they sting.

This results in their death. Female worker bees can lay eggs, but because they are not mated, they produce eggs that only develop into drones. The queen's pheromone blocks the worker bees' desire to lay eggs. A hive without a queen for an extended period may have laying workers. It takes a fertilized egg twenty-one days from egg being laid until becoming a worker bee.

The drone

Drone

Drones are the males in the colony. The drone is a very large bee with large head and eyes that predominate the head. The rear of the drone is rounded. Drones cannot sting because they do not have a stinger. Drones do not have any hive duties. They have only one purpose, and that is to mate with the queen. They have a short life of luxury. The drones are welcome into any hive to get food or shelter. Therefore drones can spread disease or carry mites from one hive to another. The drones have a very short life. Once they mate with the queen, they die. The colony will only allow the female bees to stay in the hive during the winter. The females do all the work, and the drones are not needed during the winter. The drones die after they are evicted in the fall. The colony reduces its size because food will be short in the winter. New drones will be made in the spring. It takes an unfertilized egg twenty-four days from the egg being laid until becoming a drone.

Honeybee facts

Honeybees were brought to America in 1621. The study of beekeeping is called apiculture. The area where the bees are kept is called an apiary. There can be over sixty thousand bees in a single colony (hive). Each colony has only one adult queen who can live two to three years. The average life of a worker bee is less than forty-five days (during the summer). The wings of the foraging workers become frayed and continue to deteriorate until they can no longer fly. A strong colony can produce sixty pounds of honey in a season. Sixty pounds is a little less than five gallons. Every pound of honey produced requires nectar collection from visiting two million flowers. Bees produce one pound of wax for every ten pounds of honey.

Honey being stored in the comb

Why do bees make honey? Honeybees make honey as a way of storing food to eat over the cold winter period. Honey is ideal for bees because it is full of nutrients and high in sugars. It is very high in energy, which the bees use to keep the cluster warm. The beekeeper's job is to make the bees feel an urgency to store more honeys than they need. This extra honey is removed for the beekeeper's use.

Bee Tongue

What is honey? Honey gets its start as flower nectar. Forager bees use their long tubelike tongue to suck the nectar from a variety of flowers. The nectar then enters their honey stomach. The nectar reacts with enzymes in the bee's honey stomach to form two simple sugars—glucose and fructose. Once back at the hive, they regurgitate the sugary fluid into the cells, or they pass it to other bees who put it into the cells.

Honey being relayed at the entrance

All the bees fan the sugar with their wings, which creates a draft and helps the excess water to evaporate. The sugary fluid becomes thicker as the moisture is reduced to around 18 percent. Lowering the amount of moisture to around 18 percent prevents the sugar from fermenting. The sugars become highly concentrated, preventing bacteria and fungi from multiplying. This is the reason bees can store the honey indefinitely without it going bad. The bees continue adding the sugary fluid until the cells are full. The bees place a wax cap over the cells when the honey is down to about 18 percent moisture. The wax cap seals the honey allowing it to be stored for long periods.

The sugary fluid contains plant material as well as sugar. This combination of plant material and sugar is thought to be an anti-inflammatory. Anti-inflammatories are thought to be antiaging. Many people think that honey helps their allergies because they think that honey contains pollen from flowers and trees that they are allergic to. In reality, honey contains only a small amount of pollen. The benefit that people think they are getting may be from honeys' anti-inflammatory properties.

The color and flavor of honey varies from hive to hive based on the type of flower nectar collected by the bees. Honey is good for most people. However, honey should never be given to infants because it contains live spores. Honey is mainly nectar made into sugars, so diabetics should use caution.

Is the honey that you buy good honey? Not all honey is good honey. The best honey is made from nectar that has been collected from a variety of plant sources. Most people want local honey because they think that it will help them with their allergies. It is more important to buy good honey rather than to buy local honey. Most small honey producers will have very good honey. Some large producers will also produce very good honey. However, good large producers are few in numbers. Large honey producers are under monetary pressure to produce lots of honey. Therefore these large producers add syrup to their honey, or they feed their bees sugar. These non-nectar-based sugars produce poor quality honey with little or no anti-inflammatory qualities. Some large producers are also pollinators.

Pollinators take their bees to all parts of the country to pollinate the various crops. Most pollinators must feed their bees during transport and while the bees pollinate the crops. Honey made by pollinator bees is sometimes not good enough for the bees to survive on. The honey will not be very good honey because the honey will likely be made from the bees being fed with sugar or made from nectar from only one plant source. This honey will be brought back to the pollinator's home and sold as local honey. A local upscale store stocks honey from New Zealand. Buying honey produced in a foreign country adds extra concerns. Our department of agriculture regulates what type of chemicals can be used in beehives in the United States. There are no such restrictions in many of the foreign countries. Chemicals that are used in hives are used to control mites or beetles. Also honey producers from foreign countries are notorious for adding syrup or other liquids to their honey to make more honey to sell. Buying from your local health food store may not be a good choice as well. Health food stores buy from large producers thereby increasing the chances that it will be poor honey.

It is important to know the source of your honey. Is the honey pure, or has it been diluted with syrup or some type of sweetener? Is the honey free of chemicals? Has it been harvested and stored in a clean, sanitary environment? It is hard to determine if the large producers are selling pure honey or if they have fed their bees with sugar while their honey supers were on the hive. The bottom line is to know where your honey is coming from. When in doubt, buy from the smaller producer. Use less emphasis on local and more emphasis on good, pure honey. You, as a beekeeper, should make sure that the honey that you sell is as pure as possible and without chemical residue.

Pollen being deposited in the comb

Why do bees collect pollen? The bees collect pollen from trees and flowers. The pollen is carried back to the hive on their back legs. Once back at the hive, the raw pollen is deposited into a cell near the brood nest. The bees cannot digest the raw pollen. The pollen is mixed by the bees with their enzymes and honey. The mixture goes through a fermenting-type process into what is called beebread. The beebread is used as a protein source to feed the adult bees, the queen, and the developing larvae.

Pollen stored near the brood area

Bee communication

Honeybees are efficient foragers. They send out scout bees to find the best sources of food. The scout bees return to the hive and relay the exact location of the best food source to the forager bees. The exact location is relayed to the forager bees by a dance language system. The dances are performed on the comb in the hive. The dance language allows the scout bees to provide information on the exact direction and exact distance of food sources to other hive members.

Other types of communication are done using pheromones. The guard bees give notice of an intruder to the other bees in the hive. The guard bees release an alarm pheromone, alerting all the bees in the hive to the possible danger. A large number of bees quickly exit the hive to confront the intruder. The queen continually releases a pheromone which helps organize the worker bee's duties.

Hives

• •

This book is going to focus on the Langstroth hive. It was invented in 1852 by L. L. Langstroth. This type of hive is still used by most beekeepers in the United States today. This hive is made of removable frames and is based on the principle of a 3/8 bee space. Mr. Langstroth found that bees require a 3/8 bee space in which to move around. If the space in the hive is more than 3/8 inch, the bees will fill the extra space with wax. If the space is less than 3/8, then the bees will be unable to freely move in this area and may not use it.

Langstroth hives come in three basic sizes—a nucleolus hive (nuc), an eight-frame hive, and a ten-frame hive

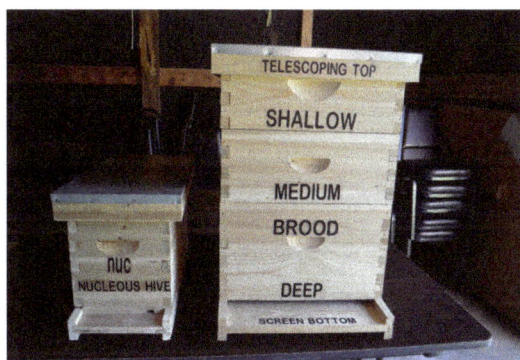

Nuc and Ten frame hive

A nuc is a five-frame hive. It is used to make splits or used to give a weak or small colony a smaller space to defend. A nuc allows a very small or weak colony a smaller space in which to grow until the colony is big enough to be placed in an eight- or ten-frame hive. Most beekeepers use ten-frame hives for more space in the hive. The added space gives the queen more room to lay, and it helps control swarming. There are many eight-frame hives in use. The eight-frame hives offer a lighter weight for those who cannot or choose not to lift the heavier ten-frame boxes. A ten-frame deep box with honey and brood weighs about eighty pounds or about eight pounds per frame. Therefore an eight-frame deep box weighs about sixteen pounds less than the ten-frame box. The downside of the eight-frame box is that there is less space. Anytime there is less space in the hive, there will be less space for the queen to lay, which may cause the bees to

19

swarm. Either the eight- or ten-frame boxes are good for the beginner. Ten-frame boxes have some advantages and is recommended for the beginner.

Parts of the Hive

Hive stands

Hives can be placed on almost anything. There are commercially made stands that can be purchased. Concrete blocks or stands made out of wood also make good hive stands. The purpose of the hive stand is to securely raise the hive about eight to eighteen inches off the ground. The distance off the ground is not critical. In fact, the bees will accept the hive even if it is sitting on the ground. Raising the hive off the ground helps keep the entrance clear. Grass may grow, and leaves or debris may blow against the hive, blocking the entrance if it were too low. Wild animals like skunks and raccoons will have to expose their sensitive underside to beestings if they have to raise up to get to the hive. Avoid using the cheaper plastic hive stands. They cannot support the weight of a heavy established hive.

Bottom boards

Bottom Boards

Solid bottom boards are the original bottom board. It was used exclusively from the 1800s until recent times. Neither beetles nor mites were a problem then. Solid bottom boards are still in use today. There are some who will tell you to never use solid bottom boards, while there are others who will tell you to not use anything else. The use of the solid bottom board is a personal preference.

The screened bottom is made in as an attempt to find a way to control mites. It has a #6 or #8 hardware cloth, covering most of the bottom. The screened bottom board has some advantages and disadvantages. Most screened bottom boards use a #8 hardware cloth. Using a #6 hardware cloth instead of a #8 hardware cloth may be somewhat better.

Some advantages are that the screen allows air to flow easier into the hive for cooling. It also may allow mites that fall off the bees while in the hive to drop out of the hive. A pan or tray may be inserted to catch beetle larva or mites that ordinarily would fall out and possibly return. The beetles and mites would drown in the oil or water that is in the pan or tray. The screened bottom board also has a slide in cover for winter or a pest management board for mite counts.

The main disadvantage of the screened bottom board is that the queen is hesitant to lay near the screened, open bottom. The open screen may allow too much light into the hive, or the queen may think that there is an opening too close to the brood area. Also too much air may enter the hive on cool evenings. The screen may allow beetle larva to have an easy exit to the ground when not using a pan or oil tray to catch them.

The slatted bottom board was originally used to increase the airflow when using a solid bottom board. Now it is also used to help make the queen more comfortable laying near the open screened bottom and to provide extra space for a hot, crowded hive. This may help reduce bearding on hot days. The slatted bottom board is also thought to allow more room for the queen when using the single brood box method. The slatted bottom board may also block some light under the frames. At very least, it moves the frames farther away from the open screened bottom.

The screened bottom board, when using a pan filled with water or oil, may be the best choice. You will be able to trap both the beetles and mites while being able to control the airflow and the amount of light entering the hive.

Entrance reducer

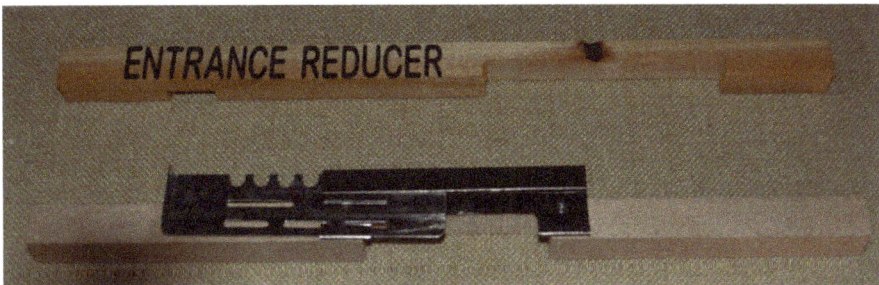

Entrance Reducers

An entrance reducer is needed to vary the size of the entrance to the hive. The entrance is reduced in the smaller colonies to improve their ability to protect the hive from intruders, such as wasps or other honeybee colonies. As the colony grows, the bees will be better able to guard a larger entrance. Therefore, the entrance size can be increased. During the main honeyflow, more bees will be coming and going. During this time, the entrance opening must be increased to alleviate overcrowding or delays at the entrance. The best time to check for entrance congestion is between three and four o'clock. This is when the majority of the foragers will be returning for the day. Do not confuse bearding with entrance congestion. Many bees will hang on the outside of the hive to cool when the hive becomes too hot and humid or there is overcrowding. This is perfectly normal and is called bearding.

Bearding

The entrance will again need to be reduced to prevent robbing after the main spring honeyflow. The main honeyflow in Southern Indiana starts in the middle of April until the end of June.

Robbing is when a stronger colony steals the honey stores from the weaker colony. The stronger colony enters the hive of the weaker colony. They kill the weaker colony, including the queen.

Sliding Metal Entrance Reducer

Reducing the entrance will allow the weaker colony the ability to fight one-on-one at the entrance instead of being overwhelmed by the larger colony. This is very important on the smaller colonies. Adjust the opening size according to the colony size. Error on the side of the entrance being too small. The new type metal sliding entrance reducer with a built-in mouse guard is the easiest to use. Mouse guards are used in the winter months to prevent mice from entering the unprotected hive. The bees will be in the cluster and not guarding the entrance.

Hive bodies or hive boxes

There are three sizes of hive boxes. The shallow box is 5 3/4 inches deep. The medium is 6 5/8 inches deep, and the deep box is 9 5/8 inches deep. The medium and shallow boxes are mainly used for the bees to store the honey that the beekeeper will remove for human consumption. These boxes are also called supers. Shallow boxes filled with honey weigh less and are used by those who do not want to lift the heavier mediums. Shallow supers weight about ten to fifteen pounds less than medium supers. The medium boxes can also be used for brood boxes for those who cannot lift the weight of a deep brood box. However, because these are smaller boxes, this greatly reduces the area in which the queen has to lay. More boxes will be required. Using medium boxes for brood boxes is not recommended for the beginner beekeeper.

Deep boxes are also called brood boxes. Many beginners get the deep box name confused with the term super because of its size. Super is the term for the honey storage box not the deeper brood rearing box. The brood boxes are used by the bees to raise their young. The queen must have plenty room to lay eggs, or the bees will swarm. The deep brood boxes provide much more surface area for the queen to lay.

Frames and foundations

Deep Frames

Medium Frames

Frames are made of plastic or wood. Foundations can be either rolled out beeswax or made of plastic. The combination of frame and foundation can be all plastic or a wood frame with a plastic or wax foundation. The frame is the structure that holds the foundation. The foundation is the double-sided, sort of flat area on which the bees build honeycomb. The bees don't have to build this surface thereby saving the bees time and wax resources. An open frame with a small piece of wax foundation or a beveled top coated with wax may also be used but will require more bee wax resources.

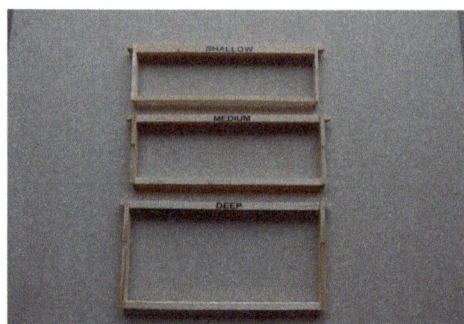

Frame sizes

The frames and foundations come in three sizes: 5 1/2 for the shallow frames, 6 1/4 for the medium frames, and 9 1/8 for the deep frames. The correct-size frame and foundation that fits the hives boxes described earlier must be used. Using a smaller frame for the bigger boxes will result in wax comb being built under the shorter frame. This will result in a mess for the beekeeper. This wax comb usually is where drone eggs are laid. Some experienced beekeepers use shorter frames as a mite control method. Drone larvae are where the mites want to lay their eggs. The comb containing the drone larvae will be cut off and discarded, taking the mite larvae out of the hive as well. However, it will be easier for the new beekeeper to always use the correct-size frames.

Plastic foundations must be coated with beeswax prior to using them in a hive.

Improper comb plastic

Bees will have a hard time correctly drawing out the comb on the plastic foundations if they are not coated with wax. Either the bees will not use the uncoated frames or they will build all kind of inappropriate comb on the frames. Wax can be applied to the plastic foundation by rubbing beeswax directly on to the frame or by heating beeswax in water and using a paintbrush to apply the wax onto the foundation. The plastic foundations have perforated corners on the lower part of the foundation. These corners can be broken off to allow an easy passage to the other side of the foundation. Bees seem to like frames with the wax foundation the best. Frames with wax foundations that are going to be used for brood must either be wired or have support pins to help the wax stay straight prior to the bees building comb. Frames with wax foundations that are going to be used in the honey super must be wired in both horizontal and vertical directions. This extra support is needed when harvesting the honey using a spinning extractor. Failure to use wired frames when harvesting your honey may result in destroyed foundations.

Frame with horizontal wires

Queen excluder

Queen excluders are made of metal—metal with a wood band or plastic. The plain metal excluder is probably the better option. However, this is a personal preference. The metal excluders have longer openings, making it easier for worker bees to pass through. The wood band is just something else to maintain. The queen excluder is placed on top of the uppermost brood box and just beneath the first honey super. The purpose of the excluder is to not allow the queen to lay eggs in the area reserved for the honey that you are going to harvest. The excluder is designed to allow the worker bees to past through but not allow the queen to pass through because she is much bigger. Some bees won't go through a queen excluder. If you experience this problem, simply remove the excluder until some of the frames are drawn out with wax comb. Don't be concerned if you wait too long to reinstall the queen excluder. After the excluder is reinstalled, the bees will hatch out, and the comb will be cleaned and then used for honey storage.

Inner cover

The inner cover is placed on top of the uppermost hive box and just under the outer cover. The deeper side of the inner cover is placed up and any notch, up and toward the front for airflow. Normally the outer cover is pushed forward in warm weather to allow airflow through the notch and pushed toward the back in the colder weather to restrict airflow through the notch. The main purpose of inner cover is to maintain the 3/8 bee space at the top of the hive and to prevent the bees from gluing on the outer cover. The inner cover also has a hole in the center that allows air to flow through the hive. The hole can be round or oblong and makes no difference which type you use. The oblong hole was originally made for the use of a Porter bee escape for easier honey harvesting. The inner cover also serves as a way to prevent intruders from entering the hive from the top especially when the hole is covered with a screen. The inner cover is also used as a place to hold a hive top feeder. A spare hive box will be required to be placed on top of the inner cover so that there is a place for the feeder.

Outer cover

The outer cover provides the hive with protection from the elements. It keeps rain, snow, and ice out of the hive. Most outer covers in use are made of wood with a top metal covering, such as aluminum. There are also covers made of plastic or all wood. Migratory covers are made of all wood and are meant to be used when transporting bees for pollination. Plastic covers can be a problem in winter. Moisture condenses on the underneath side of the cover and drips down onto the bees. Wood has insulating properties while plastic, not as much. The plastic becomes much colder than the wood, and therefore the warm moist air in the hive condenses on the plastic top much easier than the wood. It is best for the beginner to avoid using the migratory covers as well as the plastic tops.

Vent shim

A vent shim is a box placed on the top of the inner cover. This shim is only about one to three inches deep and has holes with screens on the sides. The vent shim allows air to flow through the hive in the warmer part of the year. It is usually placed on the hive around the first of June and removed in September. For maximum cooling, consider using a screened inner cover instead of a wooden one.

Moisture board and quilt box

A moisture board is made of an absorbent fiber material called Homasote. It is placed on the top box of the hive in the winter. The top box most often is a candy board or a brood box. The moisture board is used to absorb condensation at the top of the hive. The moisture board allows the hive to have limited or no airflow. A piece of insulation can also be placed on top of it to insulate the top of the hive. The warmer the top, the less chance of condensation forming and dripping on the bees. A combination of insulation and candy board will allow you to block most or all the airflow through the top part of the hive, keeping the colony warmer.

A quilt box uses wood shavings to absorb moisture. Warm moist air is allowed to flow through the quilt box. The wood shavings absorb the moisture. The problem with the quilt box that while it does remove moisture, it also allows heat to escape out the top of the hive. Neither the moisture board nor the quilt box are necessary. Insulating the top is an effective way to prevent moisture condensing on the top of the hive.

Insulating the hive

Insulating a hive can be a good thing, but too much insulation can be much worse than no insulation at all. It is a good idea to insulate the top of the hive to prevent moisture from condensing on the top of the inside of the hive. Warm air can hold much more moisture than cold air. As the warm moist air rises in the hive, it comes in contact with the top of the hive. If the top is colder than the air, condensation will form. When the warm moist air comes in contact with the cooler top, the air temperature drops. The cooler air cannot hold as much moisture as the warmer air. Therefore some moisture in the air condensates on the cooler top surface. If not, the rising moist air will fold outward toward the sides of the hive. It then turns downward along the outer sides of the hive. The warm moist air will condensate on any surface that is cooler than it is. It is better for the moisture to condense on the sides of the hive than on the top. Instead of dripping on the bees, the moisture will simply run down the sides and out of the hive and not on the bees.

There is no need to seal the cracks when installing the closer board. The entrance and any spaces in the closer board should remain open. This will allow fresh air to enter the hive without flowing through and taking heat with it. This is especially true when insulating and sealing the top of the hive.

Wrapping the hive adds even more concerns. Wrapping the hive with house wrap or some other type of paper may be okay. Avoid using plastic or insulation with a higher R value. Plastic will trap moisture either in the hive or on the outside of the hive. Over insulating the hive can cause the bees to think that it is much warmer outside than it really is. The bees may fly out thinking that it is warm enough and become too cold to return to the hive. In the winter, it may be best for the beekeepers to only insulate the top of the hive and provide some other type of windbreak for the hives. It is not necessary to wrap the hives in most areas. The only exception is to help a very small colony stay warm. This small colony should have been combined in the fall. Some consideration should be given to insulating or shading a hive that is continually in the direct sunlight of summer. These hives can easily become overheated resulting in reduced honey production. The windbreak used in the winter may be a good solution to block the hot western summer sun.

Closer board

A closer board is a board used to cover the screened bottom board in the winter. This can be made of any type of material and usually is made of corrugated plastic or thin plywood. The closer board is usually installed by the middle of October and is removed when the temperature gets warmer in late May or early June. There is no need to seal the gaps between the closer board and the bottom board when the closer board is installed in the winter. The small gap or cracks will not affect the cluster temperature and will provide air to enter the hive in the event the snow or ice blocks the entrance. An integrated pest management (IPM) board can be used as a closure board. There is very little or no difference. The IPM board has lines, and it costs more.

How Does This Thing Work?

● ●

Get your bees on order and purchase your hive, tools, and protective equipment

Order package bees, order a nuc of bees, or catch a wild swarm. Most bees are ordered in the last part of the year or the very beginning of the New Year. Don't wait until April to try to buy bees because you may not find any. The delivery will be in late April or early May. Find out before you order when you are to expect your bees. The sooner that you receive your bees, the better the chances for success. The main nectar flow starts in late April and ends in June. Feeding one to one sugar water may be necessary to help build the colony of a nuc or a package. Catching a swarm or purchasing a nuc of bees is the best option for the beginner.

A nuc of bees usually comes with four or five frames of bees with drawn-out comb. The bees already have a great start. A word of caution is to inspect the nuc of bees that you receive as soon as possible to look for signs of problems. The main issue may be queen cells. If you are unsure, ask for help. A nuc that swarms can result in a very weak colony. A beginner has a good chance of losing a weak colony. Ordering packages or nucs allows you to select what type of bee you are getting and with swarms you have to take the type of bee that you catch. The queen can always be replaced to change the bees to the type of bees that you want. Most beekeepers will advise you to buy local bees. However, most all of the bees that are being sold are not local.

Bees should be ready as early as possible in the year. The cold weather and the lack of flowering food sources do not allow quality drones to be available in our area until late April or early May. Therefore most queens are raised in the warmer southern states and are paired with splits made from bees from the southern states or bees returning from pollination in California. The only real way to get local bees is to catch a wild swarm. Catching a swarm doesn't mean that you are getting wild bees. The bees may have come from a nearby beekeeper. Most wild swarms are very good bees. Catching swarms is very easy and will be covered later. The advantages of catching swarms are cost and colony growth.

Swarms cost very little compared to purchasing a nuc or package. The biggest advantage of catching a swarm is the swarm's ability to rapidly build wax comb. The swarming bees are mostly younger bees and have prepared by filling themselves up with honey from their hive before taking flight to swarm. These younger bees are efficient comb builders. Swarms will usually grow much faster than nucs or package bees and may even produce honey in their first year. This is a great option for the beginner. Anyone can catch bees even the most inexperienced beekeeper. Catching your first swarm will bring many good emotions to the beginner. The bees are free!

Should you purchase or build a hive. It may be best to purchase your first hive. However, you can build some or all of your hive. Check the cost of both ways because by the time you purchase all the supplies that you need, it could cost as much or more as buying everything. You will need a bottom board, entrance reducer, two deep brood boxes, queen excluder, one or two supers, an inner cover, an outer cover, and enough frames with foundations to fill the brood and supers. Some type of feeder may also be needed. Don't be afraid to make some parts of your hive if you have the equipment and the skills. There are many plans with dimensions on the internet. It is a part of the beekeeping experience.

Protective equipment needed will be a bee jacket or full suit and gloves.

Gloves

The key in determining whether to purchase a jacket, suit, or both is your comfort level around bees. A jacket instead of a full suit is usually all you need. The stinger on the honeybee is short and usually will be too short to sting through thicker jeans or work-type pants. Don't be ashamed or feel less of a beekeeper for wearing a full suit. A properly worn full suit offers an almost complete assurance that you will not get stung most of the time. You must develop a comfort level around bees. However, a full suit can be hotter than a jacket. Purchasing less defensive bee will help some.

When in doubt, purchase the full suit and then purchase a jacket later when you are more comfortable around the bees. You can always use the suit if you decide to catch wild swarms. Always use some type of protection especially on your face around your eyes. Getting stung in the sensitive areas around your eyes can not only be more painful than other area of your body, it may also result in your eye swelling shut for a good part of a day or overnight. A beginner should always suit up before working with a hive. There are two basic types of suits and jackets and many variations of them. One being a fully ventilated and the other being a cotton and polyester blend nonvented jacket or suit.

At first, you may think that the vented jackets and suits are the best. However, the solid cotton and polyester jackets and suit may be lighter in weight and may be more comfortable. The beginner should try both types if possible before buying a suit or jacket. All beginners should wear gloves especially until learning how to handle the bees. There are bee gloves available in many types. Most beekeepers, including beginners, may want to use the 9 mm nitrile gloves. Nitrile gloves have several advantages. Every type of gloves will become soiled with honey and wax making them no longer useable. Nitrile gloves are cheap. If they get dirty, simply put on another pair. The gloves can be tossed after every use if needed. This will lower the risk of spreading any diseases if you go to hives other than your own. The biggest advantage of the nitrile gloves is that they allow the beekeeper better control when picking up frames.

Better control means the beekeeper can be more gentle, making things easier. The only downside is that the nitrile glove tears easily, and the bees may at times sting through them. This does not happen very often. Use the smoker to coat the gloves with smoke and the bees will stay away from them. The beginner may want to try nitrile gloves before buying regular bee gloves. Almost all bee suits and jackets have elastic straps at the end of both sleeves. These straps are placed around the index finger to prevent the sleeve from pulling back, exposing the wrist area when working with bees. The straps also make it much easier to put on the normal bee gloves because they hold the sleeves down so that the gloves can be pulled over the top of the sleeves.

Suggested tools

The suggested tools that you may need are a smoker, some type of smoker fuel, a hive tool with a small hook, a frame rest for hive inspections, a bee brush, a mite check container, uncapping roller, a double honey filter, and a swarm box. The hive tools with the smaller hooks are the easiest to use. Other tools are available and may make things easier, but these are the basic tools. It is important for the beginner to have all the necessary equipment and supplies to check and treat for mites. This is the main reason that beginners lose their colonies. Therefore a mite check container is essential. Some beekeepers will say that a brush is not needed. However, the brush can be used by the beginner to gently move bees out of harm's way when working with the various hive parts. The bee brush will also be useful to remove the bees from the honey super frames prior to harvest. There are several ways to uncap honey.

Uncapping Roller

The cheapest and by far the easiest way to uncap honey is by using an uncapping roller.

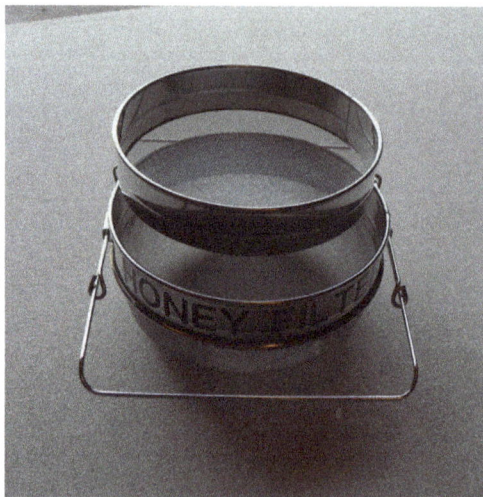

Double Honey Screen

A double screen honey filter is the only filter that is needed to clean your honey before bottling. Every beekeeper should have at least one swarm box. A swarm box will catch your bees if they swarm and can be used to catch other swarms. The swarm box doesn't have to be fancy. Most beginner beekeepers can build a swarm box for themselves. It is only a temporary home for the swarm. The beginner may want to purchase everything in the picture.

Smoker fuels

A smoker is used to calm the bees by blocking the guard bee's alarm phero-mone. Give two to three puffs of smoke at the entrance. Wait a minute or so and then proceed with your task. Open the hive and give a couple more puffs of smoke as the inner cover is being removed. Extra smoke may be given to keep the bees clam. Do not over smoke because it will not serve any useful purpose. Smoking too much will make it harder to find some queens. The queen may hide from the smoke. Lighting a smoker can seem difficult, but it is very easy. To light a smoker, simply place small pieces of cardboard into the bottom of the smoker.

Either peel one side of the cardboard off or use a small piece of paper to start the cardboard pieces on fire. Puff the smoker until there is a hot flame. Pack the smoker with fuel, such as pine needles, wood chips, or most anything of this nature. Close the smoker and pump the bellow. Add additional fuel as needed. No need to relight when refueling. The smoker can be extinguished by placing a cork or piece of wood in the small hole where the smoke comes out. This will cut off the air supply, and the fire will go out saving any remaining fuel in the smoker. There's no reason to spend lots of money on smoker fuel. There are many low cost or free options.

Next ready your hive for use. Most hive parts need to be painted to protect them from damage from water and the sun. Paint the entire exterior of the hive. The top, if aluminum, will not need painting. Paint only the exterior of the hive. Do not paint the inside or upper and lower edges of the hive boxes. Don't worry if a small amount of paint gets on the edges. Paint the bottom board but not the screen if using a screened bottom. Have fun with your hive. The hive can be painted most any color, or add any type of decorations as desired. Avoid the dark colors such as black or dark brown or blue as these colors may cause the hive to get to hot. Personalize your hive with flowers and decorations. Don't forget handprints if you have youngsters. Make memories and keepsakes. Have fun with this project!

Choose a location

The best place to set you hive is where it can face the east or southeast. The bees like the shady areas the best. However, the beetles like that as well. Therefore, it is best to place the hive in a sunny area. The bees can tolerate the sunny area better than the beetles. The most ideal location is where the hive receives the early morning sun on the front of the hive, mostly sunny all day, and then where the very hot western afternoon and evening sun is partially if not totally blocked. Also the cold winter winds will blow from the north, hitting the back of the hive and not directly into the hive entrance. A wind block from the north or west is ideal in winter. The same wind block can be used to block the hot western sun in the summer. The sun in the winter will be coming from the south, allowing the sun to warm the front entrance in the winter. This will help with cleansing winter flights.

Everyone will not have the ideal location. Place the hive as best you can. The bees will adapt to whatever position that you put them. This may cause a little extra work for the beekeeper because of beetles, or it may not be an issue at all.

Water source

A nearby water source is also important. A lake, pond, ditch, or water fountain are great water sources. Take care if neighbors have a swimming pool. A water source must be provided for the bees, or your bees will be unwelcome visitors at the neighbor's pool. Always be a responsible beekeeper. Some people feed the hummingbirds. This can also be a source of problems because the bees like the hummingbird's sweet food. Some types of hummingbird feeders leak when they are tilted slightly by the wind. This type of feeder will cause the person feeding the hummingbirds to have to continually fill their feeder. When the person sees the bees, they will think that the bees are consuming all the food when it is really just running on the ground. The sweet water will attract your bees, causing them to get blamed. A possible solution is to replace the hummingbird feeder with the type that resist leaking when tilted. Always try to find a solution if possible.

Choose the location before your bees arrive. Place your bees within three feet of the location that the bees are going to reside before releasing them. The bees learn the exact location and not which hive that they live in. The bees can be trapped in the hive at dark and moved to the new location. The next morning, the bees can be released after placing some type of restriction in front of the entrance. A tree branch or towel can be used as a restriction. Otherwise the bees will have to be trapped in the hive for two days prior to releasing them at a new location that is less than one mile from the original location. The forager bees will go back to the original location if they are moved to a new location a short distance away without taking precautions. The bees remember the location not which hive.

Setting up your hive

It is important to get the hive reasonably level from side to side. The hive can be titled slightly forward to prevent rain or snow from running into the hive. Bees draw comb using their built-in level. Therefore an out-of-level hive can result in wax comb that connects one frame's wax foundation to another. You will start setting up your hive by placing the bottom board on some type of hive stand. This can be concrete blocks, a wooden frame, or a stand that you purchased. The stand doesn't have to be pretty, but it has to be strong enough to hold the heavy weight of a full hive. Next you will add a deep hive body with enough frames to fill the box. Add the entrance reducer. Place the inner cover on top of the deep brood box and then the outer cover. Simple enough. You are ready for your bees.

Installing your bees

Installing your bees will be very easy if you purchased a nuc of bees or captured a swarm in a proper swarm box. After suiting up, simply open up your hive and take out frames from the center of your hive. Take out two more frames than the number of frames in the nuc or swarm box. Carefully move the frames from the nuc or swarm box into your hive in the same order and direction as they were in the nuc or swarm box. Place the two extra frames back into the hive. Gently slide the frames together until the sides of the frames are touching each other. The frames should be in the center of the hive box with the remaining space equally divided on both sides.

Be careful not to smash any of the bees, especially the queen. Dump any remaining bees into or in front of the hive. Replace the inner and outer cover. Feed one to one sugar water to help the bees build wax comb and to store a small amount of honey. Swarms do not require feeding. Discontinue feeding when the bees either stop taking the sugar water or when the bees are filling the brood area with honey. Feeding is only required for a short time. Never add lemongrass oil to a hive where a nuc or swarm is being transferred to. The lemongrass oil will more than likely result in the bees moving out of their new home.

Install package bees by opening up the hive and removing two frames. Dump the bees into the hive. Replace the two frames that were removed earlier. The package will come with a queen that is new to the other bees. She will be in a cage with a cap and a candy plug. Remove the cap if it has one, but do not remove the candy plug. Place the caged queen on a frame in the hive, cage, and all. The other bees must get used to the queen, or they will kill her. It will take the bees some time to eat the candy out to release the queen. This will be enough time for them to get acquainted with her. Check to make sure that the queen was released after a few days. If not, release her into the hive.

How to catch a swarm

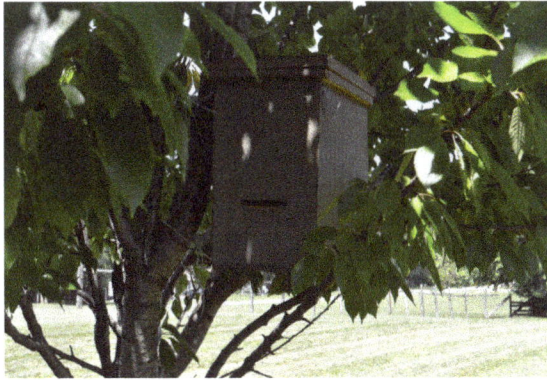

Swarm box in tree

Swarms can easily be caught in our area from April until Fall. However, as the season progresses, the swarms get smaller. Swarms caught after the middle of June will have a hard time growing and storing enough honey to make it through the winter. It is best to catch a swarm in April through the end of May. Bees start to swarm in Southern Indiana in April, while most wild bees swarm in the middle of May. Catching a swarm in the middle of May is almost a 100 percent guaranteed. Catching a swarm is very easy. There is no need to go looking for bees because with a swarm box, they will move into your swarm box. Almost any type of bucket or box can be used to catch a swarm. The difference is how easy it is for you to get the bees from the swarm trap into a hive. Don't make extra work for yourself. Use a swarm trap that has the normal deep frames with no extra space around the frames (only 3/8 bee space).

This is accomplished by using a swarm box that is designed to hold five or six deep frames. Many will say that the frames in the swarm box must have drawn comb on them. This is not the case. The answer to catching bees is to place five or six drops of lemongrass oil directly on top of the wood frames that are in the swarm box. Wood frames work best because the lemongrass oil will be absorbed by the wood frame, but plastic frames will work as well. A drop or two may be added to the box near the entrance. Too much lemongrass oil on the front may cause the bees to move onto the outside of the swarm box instead of on the frames inside.

There is no need for a Q-tip or baggie as most suggest. Forget this method. Place your swarm box on a small limb, in a tree about five or six feet off the ground. Secure the box to the tree with strings or a rope. It usually takes four or more short strings to secure the box to prevent tipping when it gets heavier. The tree doesn't need to be a huge tree and should not be in the woods. The tree should be near an area with flowering plants that are going to bloom and/or near a water source. Flowering trees in April will be loaded with bees. Placing your swarm box in this type of tree probably will not be successful. The bees are taking this nectar back to their hive until the hive becomes overcrowded with bees and honey. The colony will soon swarm. Place the swarm box in the general area but not necessarily on the flowering tree. It is better to place the swarm box a distance from the flowering tree. Never place honey or sugar water in or near your swarm box. Like the flowering tree, the sugar or honey will attract robbers and not a swarm. Also ants will fill the swarm box if the sugar or honey is placed into the swarm box.

Paint the swarm box a color that will blend in so that it won't easily be seen. It can be most any color, including green or brown or even camouflage. Use exterior paint that is available or can be purchased at a low cost. The color is not really important. The color is used to blend in to help prevent theft. The best entrance for a swarm box is a slot that is a half inch by four inches wide. The slot is easily made with a half inch drill bit and a saw. Round entrances allow birds or mice to enter. These openings require a cross wire or mesh over the opening.

The swarm box can also be hoisted high in a tree with a rope. This method will work, but it is not necessary. The swarm box with bees will become very heavy. A lite box goes up, and a heavy one must come down. There is absolutely no reason to risk getting hurt by using a tall ladder. There is no need to go high. Lemongrass oil is the only attractant that you need. I believe that lemongrass oil encourages bees to swarm. Lemongrass oil can be purchased on the internet, from beekeeping supply stores and from most health food stores. Find the cheapest source. They all work the same. Don't be fooled into believing that you need some of the other types of swarm lures. They all have lemongrass oil in them and other ingredients that make you believe that you must use their attractant to catch bees. The other ingredients are used to catch your money. Don't be fooled!

Some very good swarm boxes have extra room under the frames to make a new swarm think that the box is big. This is a very good design. However, the bees will build wax comb under the frames if they stay in the box too long. You should leave the bees in the box for at least a week but no more than three weeks. When the bees swarm, they are ready to build comb. They are full of honey and can quickly fill a five or six frame swarm box. A very good swarm may even swarm out of that swarm box in a matter of three to four weeks.

Not sure if you have a good place to catch a swarm? Look for bees on flowers. If you see honeybees, then it is a good location. There's a very high probability that you will catch a swarm.

Some state's department of natural resources agencies maintains a swarm list available to the public. Add your name to the list, and someone who has a swarm on their small tree or bush may call you. There may be other swarm lists in your area.

Feeding the Bees

As a general rule, feeding one to one sugar water in the spring should be limited to a weak hive, such as a nuc, split, packages, or a hive that did not do well in the winter. These weak hives will not receive a honey super until the colony is stronger and feeding is discontinued. Feeding sugar water will greatly increase the chance that your bees will fill the brood area and cause them to swarm. Use caution not to overfeed. Keep feeding your weaker hives until the heavy nectar flow is in progress. There should be enough available food for most strong colonies. Also use caution when using a feeding stimulates.

Feeding stimulates may cause robbing by stronger neighboring hives. The beekeeper should never feed when the honey supers are on the hive. The result will be honey made from sugar, instead of honey made from plant nectar. Never feed any type of sugar water after temperatures drop in November through March. This will result in too much moisture in the food and can cause the bees to have health issues. Candy boards and dry sugar are better for the bees during this time.

One to one sugar water means eight pounds of sugar to one gallon of water. One gallon of water weighs about eight pounds. This concentration is used for the bees to raise brood and to build wax comb. It is used in the spring to build up nucs, splits, or weak colonies. It is also used in the period of July and August to provide for the weaker colonies to help them survive and build up in the event of limited or no natural nectar source. Also the bees must be fed if the beekeeper removed too much honey. Always check to see how much honey is in the brood box before removing the honey supers for harvesting. Lift the brood boxes to make sure that they are not real light. The frames can also be removed to visually check for honey. The bees must have food when there isn't any natural nectar available. The bees count on the stored honey for food at this time. The bees will die if the beekeeper removed too much honey. One to one is also fed in September and October to build brood for winter.

Never overfeed because this will usually result in swarming. Swarming will defeat your purpose for feeding. Overfeeding will result in the bees filling too much brood area with honey. The acceptable amount of honey stored in the brood area varies from spring to late fall. In the spring, the queen will be laying at full capacity. She must have as much room to lay as possible. The stored honey should be limited to an upper crown of honey just above the brood area. This is mainly seen in the upper brood box. In the fall, the queen laying is greatly reduced or ceases for a short time. The entire brood box can be filled with honey in preparation for winter.

Two to one sugar water is used for winter preparation. Two to one means sixteen pounds of sugar to one gallon of water. This concentration is used for the bees to make honey. It is used in the late fall to help the bees store enough food for winter. This is very important when harvesting the fall flow. When using a double brood box, the goal is to have the bees fill the entire top brood box. A limited amount of honey should be stored in the bottom brood box. The bees will start the winter in the bottom brood box. The bees must only fill the top box. Filling both boxes can cause a late swarm which will defeat your efforts of getting your bees ready for winter. The queen must have room to lay, or the bees will swarm. The only way to recover from a late swarm is purchasing a queen because there won't be enough time for the bees to make a quality queen.

Types of feeders

Entrance feeders may be used if there are only one or two hives. Entrance feeders are not only easy to fill but also it is easy to see when they need to be filled. The only downfall of the entrance feeder is that it may cause bigger colonies to rob and kill the smaller colonies that you have the entrance feeder on. Avoid using feeding stimulates, such as Honey B healthy, when using entrance feeders around a location with multiple hives. This includes any neighboring beekeepers and wild colonies.

Top feeder. There are many types and sizes of hive top feeders. Theses can include the plastic round or rectangular feeders or a glass quart jar with tiny holes in the top. The hive top feeders are placed in a spare honey super (with the frames removed) which has been placed on top of the inner cover. The hive top feeders are usually larger and can hold more liquid food. They don't have to be filled as often.

Frame feeder. Frame feeders are installed by removing one of the outside frames and replacing the removed frame with a frame feeder. The feeder is filled with either one to one or two to one sugar water. It is extremely important to place some type of floating material, such as small pieces of wood or wood chips, in this feeder to prevent the bees from drowning. A cap and ladder system can also be used in the frame feeder, but it must be assembled and used properly. This type of feeder should be avoided by the beginner beekeeper as it will usually result in the bees dying due to drowning. Make sure that you know how to use this type of feeder before adding one to your hive.

Candy board. A candy board is a feeder that is used to feed dry sugar or a sugar mixture in the winter. The sugar mixture is poured into the board and hardened before it is placed on the hive. The candy board helps in two ways. One it absorbs excess moisture in the hive. Second it provides a great food source for the bees during the winter. Dry sugar can be placed on wax paper or newspaper instead of the sugar mixture. The candy board is placed directly on top of the frames of the top brood box. The candy board is like an insurance policy. It gives protection against a low food supply food and moisture in the hive.

Community feeders. A community feeder is usually a larger feeder that is placed in a location away from the hives. Feeders should be placed several hundred feet away from the hives to prevent the start of robbing. There are several types of community feeders. There are bucket-type feeders, chicken feeders with rocks or sticks to prevent drowning, an open-type feeder with straw or wood chips to prevent drowning, and a multi-jar-type feeder.

The problem with community feeders is that once they are used, they must be continually used until a good nectar flow becomes available. Otherwise there is a very good chance for robbing. The forager bees will become accustomed to having an easy food source. When this easy food supply ends, they seek another easy source. Larger colonies will attempt to steal the weaker colonies' honey. In the process, the weaker hive will be killed. Also the beekeeper cannot regulate which colony is taking the sugar water. This sugar may end up in your honey, or a colony will fill their hive with honey and swarm. The open type of feeder is used by some larger beekeepers. This is how large beekeepers make lots of honey. Honey made from sugar that is! Community feeders can be a source of disease or sickness if not cleaned frequently. Mold and bacteria can grow in the sugar water. Beginners should avoid using community feeders. I believe that community feeders are a bad choice for all beekeepers.

The community feeder can be used in the fall to get the colonies ready for winter. Feeding stimulates with essential oils can be used. The cold temperature will provide a feeding-ending point, reducing the issue with robbing. The larger colonies will dominate. The weaker colonies may not get the food that they need. Therefore an in-hive feeder for the weaker colonies will still be needed.

Pollen patties

There are two types of patties. Each is serving a specific purpose.

Winter patties contain mainly carbohydrates and about 4 percent protein. Almost all the patty is digestible by the bees. These patties are used to feed some protein to the bees. They are used from November through early February. Using higher protein patties or substitutes in the winter can cause an unwanted increase in brood. The higher protein patties also contain materials that the bees cannot digest and can result in the bees excreting in the hive causing disease. The bees cannot fly outside during periods of inclement weather for their cleansing flight.

Brood patties contain much more protein. They are used so that the queen will be fed more protein to ramp up her egg laying. Brood patties are fed in late February or early March to increase brood production. The brood will become foragers for the spring nectar flow. They are also used in September to increase brood production for increasing the number of bees for winter. Colonies located near trees will normally have adequate pollen supply during the February through March period. Feeding too much pollen can result in the producing too many bees too early in the spring. Large population of bees will consume large amounts of the honey stores. If the supply gets low or exhausted, the colony will die. The colony may attempt to swarm too early. Beginners may want to avoid feeding brood patties until becoming familiar with swarm prevention. Brood patties are not essential for the colony to survive.

The best time to work with the bees during the spring is midmorning to late afternoon and earlier as the season turns warmer. This is the time that many of the foragers will be out collecting nectar resulting in the lowest number of bees in the hive. Less bees in the hive means less bees to deal with. Warm, sunny, and calm days are best. Avoid windy, rainy, cold days as well as early morning, late evening, or after dark. During these times, the hive has the largest number of bees in it. The bees aren't very happy when they are cramped up and cannot perform their normal tasks.

Working with the Bees

Inspect your hive every two weeks in the spring. The main goal is to make sure that the queen is productive and laying and there are no problems in the hive. The colony should be getting stronger and bigger. Watch for sign of swarming (queen cells), and look for problems or signs of disease. Determine if an extra brood box is needed if there is only one or if more supers are needed.

A productive queen will lay a solid pattern of eggs which become brood. One of the goals of the hive inspection is to make sure that the queen is laying a solid pattern a of worker larva. The larva must not be in a spotty scattered pattern. The worker larva is much smaller than the drone larva. It is easy to see the difference. Drone cells should not be mixed with the worker larva. Drone larva are usually near the bottom and corners of the frames. A mixture of worker larva and drone larva in the pattern is an indicator of a problem with the queen.

Checking the hive often will allow the beekeeper to know if the colony is preparing to swarm. Swarming can be stopped if all the queen cells are found and destroyed before the eggs are laid. Removing queen cells after an egg is laid in any one of them may result in a queenless colony. Use caution and seek advice if you are unsure. Once a swarm is triggered, it is almost impossible to stop. At this point, the only way to stop a swarm is to make an artificial swarm. An artificial swarm is the same as doing a split. This type split requires that the old queen be removed from the original colony.

There are several types of diseases that the honeybee can get. For the most part, the beginner probably will not experience any of these. The key to the health of the colony is to have adequate mite control, knowing when and what to feed. Avoid feeding honey from other colonies. Honey contains live spores. Some can contain spores of foul brood and other diseases.

The final concern of the hive inspection is to make sure that the colony is growing. A good queen will be laying over a thousand eggs per day. This should result in colony growth. Notes or a record will make it easier to remember the information from an inspection especially if inspecting more than one hive. If the colony is not growing, find out why. Possibilities are a poor queen, high mite infestation, the bees swarmed, a food shortage, or a disease or sickness. Ask for help if unsure.

Protective equipment

A beginner should always wear a protective suit and gloves when working with bees. If you work with bees, you will get stung. After a few stings, this won't be as big an issue. It seems like the beekeeper builds a resistance to the bee venom, making it hurt less after each sting. You will simply become more careful andhave less fear. Most people automatically say that they are allergic when they are really not. Allergies can range from mild to severe. Mild means swelling in localized area of sting. Severe means anaphylactic shock (tongue or throat swells, trouble breathing, etc.). The best precaution is an EpiPen (epinephrine) if you know that you are allergic. A simple blood test is available if you're concerned.

Avoid being stung in the face especially around the eyes. This is a very sensitive area. Getting stung near the eye will more than likely cause your eye to swell shut. This is not something to automatically be concerned about. Use common sense when determining if you need professional help. For most people, the swelling will be for a short period, such as overnight. The pain and swelling can be lessened by limiting the amount of venom that is injected. When a honeybee stings, it rips out the venom sac along with the stinger. The venom sac will continue to inject venom until it is removed, or the sack is emptied. This process can be quickly stopped by scrapping the stinger and sack off the skin. Never squeeze the sack as it will inject all the remaining venom.

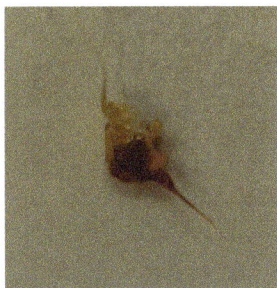

Honey Bee Stinger
with venom sac

Adding a brood box

If you are using the two-brood method with ten frames, you must add a second brood box when the first brood box has about seven to eight frames filled out with comb. Two frames of brood are going to be removed from the middle of the existing brood box and moved into the center of the brood box being added. This will encourage the bees to move up into the newly added brood box. To add a brood box, remove the inner and outer covers. Remove three of the middle frames of the brood box that you are going to add. Next carefully remove two frames of brood and eggs from the center of the existing brood box.

One at a time, place each one into the space in the box being adding. Then place one of the frames that you removed from the box you are adding to fill the box. Place the other two empty frames into the existing brood box. Place the box you are adding onto the top of the existing box. Replace the inner and outer covers. An extra frame is removed from the box being added so that there would be less chance of damaging the brood or bees on those frames. Be extremely careful to not harm the queen. In the spring, it may be advantageous to add a honey super or two when adding a brood box. This will help with swarm prevention.

How to do a brood box rotation

Brood box rotations are a method of swarm control. If you aren't concerned about your bees swarming or if you plan on catching your swarms, this rotation can be disregarded. Experienced beekeepers know that the swarming bees greatly reduce honey production as more than half of the younger bees leave to form a new colony.

There will be two-brood box rotations—one in early March and another in early April. Before rotating the brood boxes, make sure that the cluster is not in both the top and bottom brood boxes. Look in the top of the bottom brood box to see if there are any eggs or larva. Do not rotate if you see eggs or larva in the bottom box. The temperatures in March and April can have some very cold days.

Therefore the cluster must not be split when the temperature is below fifty degrees or if it is raining. After verifying the cluster position, simply move the top box below the bottom box. The first rotation takes the empty or mostly empty lower box and moves it to the top, making the bees think that they have more room. The bees will again make their way back up into the top box. The second rotation again moves the bees to the lower box and provides extra space on top. During the second rotation, the honey supers are added. The combination of rotating the boxes and adding the supers will stimulate the colony to get working.

Adding a honey super. In the spring, the number of honey supers that are added depends on the population of the colony that the supers are being added. Two supers are added for a larger robust colony and one super for a new or smaller colony. The larger colony will quickly fill a super during the main nectar flow. The bees may need some encouragement to start using a super with new foundations. The use of frames and foundations with drawn comb will speed the bee's acceptance of the super. Therefore if frames with drawn comb are available, place at least two frames in the center of the super being added. The more frames with drawn comb, the better.

Add a queen excluder to the uppermost brood box. Then add the super on top of the excluder. Add the second super on top of the first one if adding two supers. If you do not have drawn comb and your bees are not building on the new foundations, try removing the queen excluder for a short time. Allow the bees to build a small amount of comb and then reinstall the excluder. No worries if the queen starts to lay in the super. Just move the queen back to the brood box and install the excluder. The eggs will hatch, and the bees will clean out the comb. The cells will then be used for honey storage. You can also try spraying the foundations with a small amount of sugar water to encourage them to go up through the excluder.

Another super will be added when the bottom super has seven to eight frames of capped honey. Monitor the growth of the colony with the one super to see if you need to add two supers on the next round of adding supers. Add a second super under the first super. A frame or two of capped or uncapped honey should be placed in the center of the super that is being added.

Adding a third super starts by rotating the first and second supers added earlier. A frame or two of capped or uncapped honey should be placed in the center of super 2. Then add the third super on top. Always keep an empty super on the very top to encourage the bees to work harder.

A fourth super is added in a similar method. First move super 3 under supers 1 and 2. A frame or two of capped or uncapped honey should be placed in the center of super 3. Then add super number 4 on the very top of super 1. Keep in mind the end of the main honeyflow in your area. For Southern Indiana, the main flow ends in late June. Adding supers near the end of the main flow may not be necessary. Always be aware of the weather and the amount of rainfall. More rain will extend the nectar flow. Adding supers will encourage the bees to collect as much nectar as possible. This will result in more honey for the beekeeper.

Hive Management

When we think of hive management, we think of pest management, disease, swarming, etc. In reality, it is all of these plus more. Hive management is the yearlong anticipation of what the bees are doing and what environmental conditions are influencing them—good or bad. Hive management means that we help the bees by doing things that will make it much easier and better for the bees to perform their daily tasks while controlling problems. There will be many tasks that are not by nature but are very similar to what occurs naturally. The bee populations are being reduced worldwide. So it doesn't matter that we help the bees as long as we stay as close to natural as possible. As an example, don't use antibiotics unless absolutely necessary. Don't use any chemicals or feed sugar when the bees are storing honey for human use. Hive management is not performed strictly by month and day but rather by temperature, rainfall, and available pollen and nectar sources.

Before you can plan your hive management, you must decide your purpose in raising bees—raising bee for honey, for bees, or to help save the bees. Raising bees to help save the bees doesn't mean that you can just place a hive in your yard and do nothing else. The hive must remain healthy by treating for mites and beetles. Failure to do so will hurt the bees instead of helping the bee population. An untreated colony will become a breeding area for mites and beetles. Mites and beetles will destroy colonies.

Next you have to decide if you are going to use one or two brood boxes. It may be easiest for the beginner to use the two-brood box method, but you certainly can use either one.

Brood box methods

Two-brood boxes. The new trend toward one brood box is based on colony losses in February and March. The colony losses are thought to be a result of too much space that the bees must heat or that they may cluster away from their stored honey. The real issue is that the bees are unable to store enough food for winter. The beekeeper did not make sure that the bees had adequate food stores. The beekeeper must understand how to use the double-brood box method. The double brood box starts as a single brood box and food storage box in the late fall. As the winter food is consumed, it becomes a double brood box by spring.

During February and March, brood numbers are rapidly increasing. Double brood boxes tend to have larger bee populations which require more food to support the large colony. Food stores can be quickly depleted. Therefore these larger hives without adequate food stores will die due to starvation. However, if you make sure that these colonies have plenty of food, you will be rewarded with a more robust hive that will be available for the main spring honeyflow. Having enough food may even help prevent swarming in April. Two brood boxes will provide more room for the queen to lay eggs, more room for food storage for winter, and more bees and lowers the chance for swarming in the spring. Also having two brood boxes allows the bee to cluster farther away from the bottom and farther away from the entrance. The cold air at the entrance and bottom will have less effect on the winter cluster.

The problem with the two-brood box method is that too much honey is removed too late in the year. Beekeepers, who sell their honey, want to harvest as much as possible. More honey, more money. This problem can be resolved by either allowing the bees to store all of the fall nectar flow or make sure that the bees are fed just enough two to one sugar water to fill the top brood box with honey and pollen by the first of November. I recommend that the new beekeeper harvest their honey in late June or early July and allow the bees to have the fall nectar flow.

One brood box. The use of one-brood box method or a version of it has become more popular. The one-brood box method is just like the name says one brood box. Using this method requires extra care to prevent swarming and to make sure the bees have adequate food for the winter. Fixing the food shortage can be as simple as adding a candy board to provide extra winter food if needed. The swarming issue will take a little more work to resolve. The beekeeper who uses only one brood box must not allow the bees to store very much honey in the brood box during the spring nectar flow. The queen needs plenty room to lay, if not, the bees will swarm.

Adding supers in a timely manner is very important. Always add two suppers when using this method. The two supers will make the bees think that they have plenty room. Excess honey in the brood area during the spring flow can be scratched open, and the bees will move it up into the supers. This should only be newly capped honey so that any old honey that was there when the mite treatments were done is not moved up into the supers. We must keep our honey chemical-free.

There are other modified one-brood box methods as well. These methods involve using a shallow super, medium super, or another deep. Some of these allow the queen to lay in the boxes during peak swarm season and then install a queen excluder between the brood box and the extra box. The cells will be cleaned out and used for honey after the bees hatch.

Another way is to add a queen excluder and a permanent shallow or medium to be used as a feeder box for the hive. The feeder box stays with the hive, and no honey is ever removed from it. The queen excluder is removed in the winter and reinstalled in the spring just before the main nectar flow.

One last method is to use one deep box above a queen excluder as a honey super. The deep super is added in April just before the main nectar flow. Frames of honey that are filled in the brood box can be moved into the deep above the brood box. Some of these frames can be returned to the brood box as frames of stored honey for the winter. Always use caution as to not harvest honey from the brood area because of mite treatments.

Benefits of a single brood box would include that there would be only one brood box to inspect and no heavy brood box to lift. Disadvantages of a single brood box is that there is a greater chance for swarming, not enough food for winter, and the cluster will be closer to the bottom and closer to the entrance. The cold air at the entrance and bottom board have little or no effect on the temperature affecting the cluster in a double. However, the bees in a single brood box are going to cluster closer to the bottom. Therefore the cold air at the bottom will have more effects on the winter cluster.

Mites

Mite

As a beginner, I thought that there wasn't a need to treat for mites. I thought that wild swarms didn't get treated and they survived. I soon found that my thinking was very wrong. My bees died, and so did most everyone else's bees who did not treat for mites. When wild swarms leave the old colony, they take a load of mites with them. Mites attach themselves to the younger nurse bees. A swarm has a very large number of these younger bees. Therefore a large number of mites go with the swarm. It takes a short period for the swarm to build comb, the queen to lay eggs, and for the larvae to develop. The mites don't have larvae to lay their eggs on in this broodless period, reducing the number of mites. The old colony goes broodless until the new queen starts laying and her eggs become larvae. Mites require bee larvae to lay their eggs on to multiply. This broodless period provides a reduction in mites for the old and new colonies. The new swarm carries and spreads the mites as they go.

Most new beekeepers don't know how to treat for mites, and therefore they don't treat. The majority of new beekeepers lose their bees for this reason. The new beekeeper should concentrate more efforts on knowing how to test and treat for mites than any other aspect of beekeeping. This is an absolute must!

Varroa mites are tiny insects that attach themselves to the honeybee. The mature mite feeds on the fat body of the bee. The mite injects an enzyme into the bee's body. This method is used to break down the fat cells so that the mite can suck the nutrients out of the bee and into their body to be used as food. The injecting and nutrient removal is how mites spread disease. The mites can become infected with a disease from one bee and then spread it to another.

The mature mite lays her eggs in the cells on the bee larvae. Mite eggs are laid a very short time before the cells containing bee larvae are capped. The emerging mite larva will attach itself to the bee larva and use the bee larva as its food source. This results in the deformation of the bee larva before it becomes a bee. The bee will have deformed wings and other parts. The deformities will have a serious impact on the new bee's ability to carry out her required tasks.

There is not much in the way of mite prevention. A neighboring colony can spread mites to your bees even if you do everything to prevent them. An untreated neighbor's bees or a wild colony will spread mites everywhere, including to your bees. The only way to control and limit the number of mites is with the various forms of treatments. You must treat for mites to prevent disease or damaged or weak brood.

There are several treatments for mites. Treating for mites uses different types of chemicals. Therefore these treatments cannot be used when the honey supers are on the hive to avoid contaminating the honey. Some of the treatments are Mite Away Quick Strips, Apavar, Apiguard, and others. All mite treatments must be used according to the manufacturer's directions. Failing to do so can result in your bees leaving the hive for a new home. Treating with these products while the honey supers are on will result in chemicals in your honey. Honey should never be extracted from the brood area for these same reasons.

Other methods of treatment include dusting the bees with powdered sugar and treating the bees using oxalic acid. The powdered sugar method is where the bees are covered with a light coat of powdered sugar. The bees have a grooming behavior. The bees will clean each other. As they are removing the powdered sugar, they will also remove some of the mites as well. Oxalic acid vapor is also used. A small amount of oxalic acid is placed into a vaporizer. The oxalic acid vapor is sprayed into the otherwise closed hive. The oxalic acid vapor coats the bees, including the mites. The mites can't tolerate the acid. The mites die and fall off the bees. The bees have a higher tolerance to the acid than the mites.

However, the bees must not be over fogged. Always follow the manufacturer's directions or seek advice before using. The oxalic acid in this method will not penetrate the wax capping. Therefore the mites in the cells will not be affected by one treatment. Three treatments, five days apart, will be required to successfully treat with this method. The good thing with this treatment is that the oxalic acid is cheap and easy to use. The oxalic acid is corrosive to your skin, and the vapors can cause lung damage if inhaled when using a vaporizer. Always wear protective gloves that can tolerate acid when handling the acid. More importantly, always wear a mask designed to protect you from the acid vapors when using a vaporizer. There are a few different types of vaporizers on the market. Some of these include the battery or electric-operated hand wand, expensive electric models, or some lower-cost electric models.

Oxalic acid is thought to be safe when the honey supers are on because the oxalic acid will not penetrate the honey that is capped. Since there will also be uncapped honey, the use of oxalic acid vaporizing should be avoided as long as the supers are on. It is best to delay all mite treatments until the honey has been removed. If in doubt about treating with supers on, *don't treat!*

The best times to treat for mites is before the honey supers go on in spring and after the supers are removed in the summer or fall. It is important to reduce the number of mites as much as possible at these times. The spring application will be the last treatment for a few months. The mite population will grow unrestricted during these months. Winter preparation will soon begin. The mite population must be reduced so that the bees made in September and October are as strong and healthy as possible. It is very important that these new bees are not deformed in any way. These bees are going to be the bees that survive the cold winter. The bees must be treated for mites. Don't think that mite treatment can be ignored. The result will be dead bees.

How to do a mite count and how to make a mite check

Checking for mites is an important part of beekeeping. It is easy to do and will allow the beekeeper to know when treatment is needed. Checking for mites will keep the beekeeper from stressing the colony unnecessarily by treating the colony when it wasn't needed. Only one colony needs to be checked if there are more than one colony. If one colony has too many mites, then they all will have too many mites.

There are commercially made mite check containers available. There are several good homemade containers as well. The process for checking for mites is the same basic way no matter which type of mite check container is used.

Equipment. You will need a 1/2 measuring cup, a white bucket or pan, alcohol or windshield washer fluid containing alcohol, water, and a mite wash container. This container can be homemade or a manufactured one. The results will be the same.

Open up a hive. Remove one frame or two that contains brood. The nurse bees will be used for this test, so the frame must have brood. Most of the adult mites enter the hive on the foragers. The mites leave the foragers and attach themselves to the nurse bees. The nurse bees are close to the uncapped bee larvae. This will make it easy for the adult female mite to easily enter the uncapped bee larvae to lay her eggs just before the bee larvae are capped. Take great care to make sure that the queen is not on the frame with brood. Locate the queen, or double and triple check for the queen. Shake the bees into a bucket or pan.

Tilt the pan so that the bees clump together. Scoop 1/2 cup of bees, and place them into your mite check container. Return the remaining bees to the hive. Place the hive back to normal. The 1/2 cup of bees contains approximately three hundred bees. The bees will be killed. Killing the bees may seem contrary to the beekeeper's goals. Accurately checking for mites is absolutely necessary to protect the remaining fifty to sixty thousand bees. Failure to treat for mites will kill thousands. Not checking will result in overtreating which will also kill more than the three hundred bees in this check. The colony will easily replace the three hundred bees used in this test.

How to check for mites. First make a small amount of washing fluid, or use windshield washer fluid that contains alcohol. The washing fluid is one part alcohol to four parts water. Pour enough washing fluid into the mite check container to more than cover the bees. This will instantly kill the bees. Swirl or lightly shake the alcohol for a few minutes to dislodge the mites. The bees have been killed, so make sure that most if not all of the mites have been dislodged. The commercial mite checks are the easiest to use. Follow the manufacturer's instructions. The manufacturer's instructions will be very similar to the instructions above. This test may not give an exact mite count, but it will show if treatment is needed.

Determine if treatment is necessary. The acceptable mite counts are different in April than in August. Treatments are necessary if there are three to four mites per the 1/2 cup or three hundred bees in April or May, while six to nine mites for the same 1/2 cup bees in August. The difference in the thresholds are due to not being able to treat for mites during the main nectar flow when the honey supers are on the hive. Mites can double or triple in a short period of time. Treat when in doubt but never treat when the honey supers are on.

Hive beetles

Small Hive Beetle

Beetles have become a problem in recent times. They become more noticeable starting in July. If left unchecked, the beetles will cause the colony to leave the hive. Beetles enter the hive either from the top or through the entrance. The entrance is usually guarded and is a harder way for the adult beetle to enter the hive. The easiest way for the beetle to enter the hive is through the hole in the inner cover. Simply covering the hole in the inner cover with a piece of screen can reduce the number of beetles that can get into the hive.

The beetle's reproduction cycle must be broken in order to get effective beetle control. The adult beetle enters the hive to lay its eggs in the comb. The beetle egg hatches and becomes a larva. The larva feeds on the honey until it is ready to leave the hive. The larva must return to the ground to become a beetle. Break this cycle, and there will be less beetles. Trapping and killing the adult beetles, as well as preventing the larva from entering the ground, are ways to break their cycle.

There are a number of ways to control the beetle population in the hive. Place the oil traps on the topmost box near the outside corners. The bees will run the beetles up into the corners, and the fleeing beetles will enter the oil traps and drown.

The beetle larva must return to the earth to become adult beetles. This is the area where the most effort should be given. The use of a screened bottom boards may help control mites, but it may allow the beetle larva to have an easy exit to the ground. There are several ways to prevent or limit the larva from entering the ground. Hive placement is one of these. The earth in the sunny area will become dry and hard, making it almost impossible for the larva to enter the ground. Therefore placing the hive in a sunny area will help control the beetle population. Placing tar paper or tin under the hive can also help control beetles.

The beetle larva may not be able to survive when falling out of the hive onto tar paper or tin (metal sheet) that has been heated by the sun. One of the best ways to control beetles is to use a pan with oil or sticky board. An oil pan or sticky board will catch the larva as they fall out of the hive when using a screened bottom. The larva will drown in the oil or get caught by the sticky board. Lime or rock under the hive can also be used to reduce the ability of the beetle larva from entering the earth.

A combination of the beetle control methods should be used to effectively control the beetle population. The easiest way to control beetles may be to use oil traps in the hive and an oil pan under a screened bottom. The oil pan will catch the larva, and the oil traps will catch the adult beetle.

Ants. Ants are more annoying to the beekeeper than the bees. There are several ways to combat ants. The best way is to not allow the ants to crawl up the hive stand by using a shield around the hive stand legs. Cinnamon can be placed under between the inner and outer covers. I have found that Febreze fabric spray is an effective ant killer and control. It kills the ants on contact, and the ants don't come back. Bees don't like the smell, so they stay away from it. Never use Febreze in a hive or around the entrance. Only the sides and back of the hive stand. Always use extreme caution when using any type of unapproved spray or chemicals around the hive. Beginners should use only approved chemicals or sprays.

Swarming. Swarming is the natural way the bees reproduce. It is also a way the bees use to preserve the existing colony in the event of low food stores. There are several things that can trigger a colony to swarm, such as overcrowding, a food shortage in the hive, or a queen with weak pheromones.

Most swarms in April are the day after an extended cold or rainy period usually occurring during the day's warm-up between 11:00 a.m. and 3:00 p.m. The hive will show little or no activity on the outside when it is raining. However, the interior is full of working bees that will consume food stores very rapidly. The bees will swarm even though the rainy, cold weather may not be favorable for swarming. A colony swarms when there is a very large population of bees with little food stores and/or no room to expand. They will swarm as a survival strategy. Swarms in April are usually city swarms or beekeeper swarms, caused by over or under feeding. In our area, most wild swarms occur in mid-May. Swarming in May is primarily due to overcrowding and the bees' desire to reproduce. If your bees swarm, they could swarm again in eight to sixteen days. Don't panic. The swarming bees normally will ball up in a small tree or bush. Simply shake the ball of bees into a hive or swarm box. All the bees will eventually go into the hive or swarm box. Never place lemongrass oil into the hive or swarm box when catching this type of swarm. The lemongrass oil will cause them to move out of the hive. All beekeepers should have at least one swarm box.

Time to catch some free bees with a swarm trap. See how to catch a swarm. Look for queen cells during the hive inspections. Queen cells on the bottom of the frames are a definite sign that the bees are preparing to swarm. Queen cells can be removed before the egg is laid to stop the swarming. However, once the egg is laid and the cell is capped, there is no stopping the bees from swarming. Removing a capped queen cell can result in a hive without a queen. A beginner should get help or do not remove a capped queen cell unless there are multiple queen cells. The old queen must be removed from the hive by doing a split. This is the only way to stop the bees from swarming. Swarming is a natural instinct for the bees. Therefore it can be difficult to control without swarm prevention.

Swarm prevention. There is a lot to swarm prevention. The main goal of swarm prevention is making the bees believe that there is plenty room for the queen to lay and to make the bees believe that they must work to fill empty supers with honey. Many will say that it is impossible to prevent swarming. However, to prevent or lower the risk of swarming, one must understand why bees swarm. The reason bees swarm is mostly due to overcrowding, lack of space for the queen to lay, a shortage of food, or an old queen with lower pheromones. Overcrowding occurs when the bees don't feel that they have enough physical space for the number of bees in the hive. The physical overcrowding is cured by adding more hive boxes in a timely manner. Brood boxes and honey suppers are added to increase space in the hive. The bees can also be tricked into thinking that they have more room by rotating the brood boxes in early March and again in April.

Overcrowding also occurs when there isn't enough motivation or there is poor weather for the bees to collect nectar, so they just hang out in the hive. Bees become less motivated when the queen's pheromones are weak or if the honey supers are nearly full. There isn't a sense of urgency to fill the honey supers when the bees believe that they have plenty stores. Adding supers will help keep the bees believing that they need more food stores. The queen's pheromones motivate the colony to carry out all the needed tasks in the hive. A low-queen pheromone level will cause the bees to slow down. The bees may make a new replacement queen, or they may get ready to swarm. Replacing an old queen is a good idea and will help prevent swarming.

It is impossible to control the weather. During cold or rainy weather, the bees will be confined to the hive. The hive can quickly become overcrowded by emerging young bees. The more bees, the more food that will be consumed. The fix for this is to anticipate the need for more hive space and the need for more food. Planning and anticipating the needs of the bees can't be overlooked. Adding a second brood box or a couple supers before a cold spell will help with the space issue. Food stores should be checked prior to a bad weather forecast. A full top brood box in November of the prior year will help with this. Feed if needed until the cold spell ends.

Another good way to help with swarming is to perform a spilt where the old queen is moved to a new location. The old hive will make a new queen, and the old queen will lay enough to start a new colony. The old colony won't swarm because it will take some time to make a new queen. The split with the old queen won't swarm because the colony is much too small to swarm.

Bee's Yearly Cycle

The information below is based off weather patterns in Southern Indiana. The information in this book will be referencing things that matter to bees occurring around a certain date. The weather, temperature, and available food determine when and how the bees carry out their tasks. Attend the local club monthly meetings for a guide to better timing. Ask when to do questions targeted toward an answer that explains why the need, the weather conditions, and what plants to look for in your area. The monthly references should be used as an approximate timing. Bees can't read a calendar. They go by the weather and the available nectar and pollen sources. The bees are opportunist, taking advantage of the resources made available to them by nature and by human intervention.

The bees have a yearly cycle where they must collect food and water, produce young, and reproduce by swarming. Sounds simple. It is extremely important to understanding the needs of the bees during the yearly cycle and how and when to help them. It will be easier to know how and when to do things if we know why things are done. By doing so, we as beekeepers anticipate possible issues and correct them before the issues become big problems. Beekeeping should be fun and not work. Do things on your schedule instead of fixing problems (swarms, beetles, mites, disease, etc.).

The bee cycle is going to be explained below. Try to understand why bees do certain things and the goals the bees have around each month. Their goals will include collecting food and water, raising their young, and forming new colonies by swarming and winter survival. Bees collect water for their use as well as to cool the hive. A water source is very important.

Please keep in mind that the monthly listings are made according to the weather that will likely occur at this time. Because our weather patterns change, beekeepers should be ready to adjust this calendar accordingly. Consideration should be given as to your location. The farther south that you are, the sooner the weather warms. On the other extreme, the farther North you are, the later the weather warms. As spring returns, trees and flowers will begin to bloom according to the local temperature. Therefore the areas to the south will have nectar and pollen available earlier than the areas to the north.

No matter where the bees are in the cycle, try to find out what happened to your bees if they die. Do a mite count even on the dead bees. The mites will still be on the bees. Look for signs of disease and available food stores. Any information that is learned will help in the future. Don't feel like a failure if your bees die. Almost all beekeepers lose some colonies. A beginner has only one or two hives. Losing all of them is easy because there are only one or two. Find out what happened to them. The problem usually is starvation, mites, or moisture. Fix the problem and get more bees. You will succeed.

The beginning of the bee cycle

I originally thought that the beginning of the bee cycle was sometime in late December. The queen starts laying a small number of eggs to replace some winter bees in late December or in early January. However, August is a better place to start the beekeeping year. The preparation by the beekeeper and the bees in August will strongly influence how well the bees survive and grow in the winter months to come.

The beekeeper can greatly reduce the bee's chances of getting sick by controlling the mites and by controlling when, what, and how the bees are fed. The main goal from August until November is to reduce the mite population as much as possible and to make sure that the colony has enough food for winter. This is accomplished in the two-brood box method by having the bees fill the entire top brood box with honey and pollen by the first of November. A single brood box will require feeding in the winter.

Most hobbyist and beginner beekeepers should consider harvesting their honey in late June to early July if there is honey in the honey supers. Never remove honey from the brood area. The spring honey is usually the best honey. Allowing the bees to store the fall nectar flow in preparation for winter will reduce the time and effort needed to prepare the colony for winter.

Starting the bee cycle

August

To start the bee cycle, there should be some consideration given to replace a queen more than a year old or a queen in a colony that has not grown during the year. If replacing the queen, it is advisable to requeen in August and no later than September. If you can afford to requeen your hive each year, it would be best to do so. A new queen will have much stronger pheromones to keep the bees motivated to work, and a new queen will be able to lay more eggs for a larger winter population. A colony with a new queen will have less tendency to swarm in the spring. This may be due in part that the new queen will have stronger pheromones.

Take off any remaining supers if you are going to allow the bees to store the fall flow. Check for mites if you treated in June or July and treat if necessary. There is no need to do a mite check at this time if you have not treated since spring. The bees will have too many mites. A mite check will be done later to check if another mite treatment is necessary. The colony was last treated for mites in spring around the first of April. Mites will be at their maximum simply because no treatment has been done since spring. It is very important to not allow the mites to weaken or damage the brood that are to become the winter bees. One important task is to make sure that the bees fill the top brood box with food stores before the first of November. There may be some time to feed in November, but it is much easier to be ahead instead of behind. The weather in November will be getting colder limiting when you can feed two to one for honey storage.

Smaller colonies have a lower chance of making it through the winter. Therefore it is best to combine small colonies in preparation for the fall flow. It is better to have one strong colony instead of two dead colonies. Strive for strong colonies with low-mite counts. This means lots of healthy bees to take advantage of the brief fall flow in preparation for winter. The goal is to ramp up the number of bees in preparation for winter. Feed small pieces of brood pollen patties or pollen substitutes and one to one sugar water to increase the queen's egg production. Caution, beetles also like pollen patties. You may be feeding the beetles. Powder pollen substitutes may be a better option if there is a beetle problem. Feeding too much sugar water will allow the bees to fill the brood area with honey causing a late swarm. Late swarms are counterproductive and will usually result in the loss of bees needed for winter. Virgin queens that mate late in the season are less likely to perform in the long term due to the lack of a good drone population. If the swarming colony virgin does mate and begins laying, plans should be made to replace her sometime in early spring.

This is the time of year when beekeepers are trying to decide whether to use one or two brood boxes for winter. Overwintering in a single deep is thought by some to be the best for winter survival. The idea is that colony losses in a two-brood box hive are due to too much space for the bees to keep warm and for other reasons. The real reason is that the beekeeper did not make sure that the bees had enough food stored to feed the bees until the spring flow in April. Removing the fall flow takes away the last natural chance for the bees to store food for the winter. If the fall flow is harvested, the beekeeper must replace the food stores or the bees will die in late February or March.

This is why most commercial beekeepers feed heavy in the fall. Commercial beekeepers feed two to one sugar water, corn syrup, or some type of food—the cheapest food possible. The reasoning is that they can sell the honey for more than they can buy winter food. The beekeeper should never harvest the honey out of their brood boxes because the bees need this honey for winter and the honey in the brood boxes has a good chance of being sugar or syrup honey, or it may contain chemicals from mite treatments.

Overwintering in a single brood box can also be successfully used. Feeding is usually required. Breaking a double down to a single is best when the colony is not big enough. It may also be necessary if there is a shortage of winter food. Heavy winter feeding will be required either for a smaller colony or a colony without enough food stores. Using a single brood box for a stronger colony is a personal preference. Like many beekeeping tasks, there are more than one way to be successful. However, some ways are easier for the beginner.

September. September is a continuation of completing your goal to lower the mite count and making sure that the bees store enough food to make it through the winter. Mite treatments and mite checks are a must after all supers are off. Evaluate the progress of filling the top brood box for winter. Feed if necessary. The beekeeper's goal is to maximum colony heath, have good food stores, and bees in bottom box with food above by the first of November. Perform a mite check to see if the earlier mite treatment reduced the number of mites to an acceptable level. Look for signs of disease and be aware of the health of the colony. A healthy colony is very important during this period as this is when the development of the winter or fat bees begins in most areas. The nurse bees will have fewer number of eggs and larvae to raise. These bees will have more time for themselves and will develop food reserves in their body. The fat bees will play an important role in the winter survival. The queen begins to lay the eggs that will become the workers which will help bring the colony through to the next spring. It takes sixteen days from egg to worker bee.

If the fall flow is harvested, the bees will be behind in their winter preparations. The bees need help immediately. Help the bees recover by feeding two to one sugar water until the bees fill the entire top brood box. Do not allow the bees to fill the bottom brood box with food stores. The queen must have room to lay eggs. An indication that you have accomplished this is that the bees are in the bottom box and the hive will have about seventy pounds of food stores. The weight will have to be estimated by lifting the corner or side slightly. The hive should be heavy. The goal is to fill the entire top brood box with honey and pollen by the first of November. This is an important goal. There may be a few additional warm days in November to complete this task. Stay ahead and not behind, and things will be easier.

October. Feed 2:1 sugar syrup (by weight) if necessary. The goal is to have the bees fill the upper brood chamber during the fall flow or by feeding them. This will force the queen down into the bottom brood chamber. There won't be any room in the top brood box. Be careful not to feed too much. Only allow the bees to fill the upper brood box with honey nor fill the bottom box. If you feed too much, the bees will fill the upper and lower brood chambers with honey and deprive the colony of space for brood rearing. If this happens, instead of having lots of young bees for the winter, you will have lots of older bees, and the colony will not successfully winter. Always error on the side of too much room rather than too little. Do a mite check and treatment for mites if necessary.

Winter preparation means mite control, moisture control, and making sure that the bees have an adequate food supply and food placement. The colony must have the right size hive for the number of bees. A small colony will be less likely to survive in a large hive box during the winter. A large colony will be able to extend to relocate honey into their cluster. The smaller colony will not be able to move at all. The honey must always be in or always touching the smaller cluster. If the colony is very small, combining it with another hive may be the best solution. To do this, find and remove the queen in the weakest colony. Place a newspaper, #8 hardware cloth, or screen between the two hives that are being combined. Leave the hardware cloth or screen on for two days. The bees will chew through the newspaper, uniting the colonies. This close yet apart time allows the bees to accept each other. Never combine hives directly as they will kill each other.

Install entrance reducers, mouse guards, and debris boards in screened bottom boards and provide windbreaks if possible. The bees will not be able to guard the entrance in the winter when in their cluster. The mouse guard provide holes big enough for the bees to come and go when needed but is too small for mice to enter. Do not be over concerned with sealing the bottom of the hive. It is good for the hive to have some ventilation in the bottom of the hive as a means of moisture control and a fresh air supply. Also small gaps in the bottom will allow air to enter the hive if the entrance becomes blocked with snow or ice. Be careful if you wrap your hive for winter. The sides must remain cooler than the top. This allows the moisture in the hive to condense on the sides instead of the top.

Condensation must not be allowed to drip on the bees, or they will die. It is okay to wrap your hives, but it is not necessary to wrap your hives in our area. Concentrate efforts toward moisture control and limiting airflow through the top of the hive. Insulate the top of the hive by adding a piece of one-half inch insulation on top of the inner cover. Adding a winter pollen patty in a candy board in November is a great way to ensure that the bees not only have enough food for the winter but also have a very good means of moisture control. Airflow through the top of the hive by using a quit box or holes in the top will remove moisture, but it will also remove heat from the hive as well. A sugar board and insulation will reduce or eliminate the need for airflow through the hive in the winter. Dry sugar or sugar patties instead of a candy board can be used to reduce costs if there are many hives.

Colony location is a key indicator of the available food stores. The bees should be entirely in the bottom brood box by the first of November. If the bees are able to move up to the top brood box before January, it means that they have consumed the food in the top brood box. Consider this to be an emergency. They do not have enough food stores. You must feed, or you will have a good chance of losing the bees to starvation in February, March, or sooner.

Again the goal is for the bees to have the upper brood box almost full of honey and pollen by November and the bees in the bottom brood box. The weight can be gauged by lifting the top brood box or checking to see if the frames are full of honey and pollen.

The winter cluster

Honeybees do not hibernate in winter. The bees form a cluster, clinging tightly together on the combs in the hive. The outer bees form an insulating shell that prevents excessive loss of heat. The inner cluster temperature in the nineties permits normal cluster activity, such as rearing the young and consuming food. Take care when working with the bees in the cold winter. It can take up to three days for the clustered bees to return to normal after being disturbed. A strong colony can move sideways and move its stores into its cluster under low-temperature conditions. Weaker colonies might starve with honey in the frame next to the cluster.

November. Check food stores and colony location in the hive. Your overwintering has become much more difficult if food stores are low. An indicator of low food stores is that the colony will have already moved into the top box. *Emergency!* The bees must be fed if food stores are low. Liquid feed (2:1) if temperatures permit or more likely fondant, candy boards, winter patties, dry sugar, etc. If you cannot get enough food in, consider breaking the hive down to one brood box. Candy boards and insulation are normally installed in November. Prevent winter snow and ice from blocking the entrance. Dead bees can also block the entrance at this time of year as well as later in winter when an entrance reducer is installed. Clear the entrance if it becomes blocked or restricted.

Use caution when feeding premixed patties at this time of the year. Use only winter pollen patties not brood patties. Winter patties are around 4 percent protein, and brood patties contain a much higher percentage of protein. In this period, we are feeding bees and not wanting to increase the queen laying. Make sure that the patties are mostly carbohydrates in content and have low indigestible inert contents, such as ash. The colony is approaching a period where it will be too cold for cleansing flights and food that contains indigestible ingredients makes it difficult on bees. Defecation in the hive can lead to dysentery and other diseases.

Make sure that all colonies are ready for the cold December through January temperatures and have the food necessary for this period. This is the month to make sure that you have your hives ready for winter—mites, moisture and food. Prepare your hive now so that you won't have to say that your bees survived the winter but died in early spring.

December. Consider oxalic acid vaporization treatment as the amount of brood is normally low during this period. Base your decision on temperatures above forty degrees and forecasted dry weather conditions. Only one oxalic acid treatment is necessary since there isn't any brood. Consult with an experienced beekeeper on the use of oxalic acid treatments is advised. Continue to monitor food supplies, lift the hive, peeking in if the temperature is above fifty degrees or if a food check has not been made. Be very quick when opening the hive in the winter. Food supplies must be checked. Do not allow the bees to starve. Check on the warmest day. The colony needs to be checked and observed occasionally for bee health and for adequate food supplies. Make sure dead bees do not block the entrance. The queen will start laying a small number of eggs to replace some of the older bees sometime in late December.

This is actually the beginning of the spring buildup. Feed only winter patties not brood builder patties. The cold winter weather will be around for many weeks to come. The brood build up will be slow due to a low natural food supply. Pollen will not be available for several weeks. Winter bees use the fat and protein they have stored in their bodies to feed the larva that are being produced. Winter bees are necessary for survival at this time. The brood will become the pollen foragers for when the weather allows. The winter bees will be too old to become foragers. The younger bees must be available to collect pollen when the weather allows and pollen becomes available.

The current honey stores in the colony will be used at an increasing rate for temperature regulation in the colder weather. As the weather warms, more stores are used as food for the increasing population of adult bees. Beekeepers should monitor long range forecasts to anticipate the needs of the bees. It is important to know how much honey was stored by November to plan if and when feeding will become necessary. Be aware of how much food has being consumed and the colony buildup.

January. Brood should be increasing as the queen increases her egg laying. Do not check for brood due to the cold temperatures. Just be aware that the queen is laying at this time. Consider doing an oxalic acid treatment on a warm day over forty degrees this month if none was done in December. Check food supplies. Food supplies are being consumed, but there still should be plenty. Remove any snow or ice that is the blocking entrance. Dead bees will fall to the bottom of the hive. The dead bees are immediately carried outside the hive in the summer by the worker bees. In the winter, the colony will be in a cluster, and the dead bees will accumulate on the bottom board.

On warm days, the worker bees will drag out the dead. You may notice more dead bees in front of your hives if there is snow on the ground. This is normal. The sun usually shines bright after a snow. This sunshine warms the hive allowing the bees to be able to remove some of the dead bees from the hive. The dead bees are easier to see on the white snow than if they were on the ground. A strong hive will be able to remove the dead bees during these times. However, not all colonies will be able to remove the dead immediately. They will do this later if possible. You may also see debris similar to sawdust in front of the hive. This is the wax cappings that have been removed by the bees so that they can consume the honey.

February. February and March are critical months. Rapidly increasing number of bees in the hive require much more food. It is critical that enough food is available, or the colony will die. The needed food is either honey or some type of sugar. February and March are when the majority of colonies die. This is mainly due to starvation.

Brood rearing is increasing, and occasional days of warming weather allow bees to take cleansing flights and clean out their home. Food supplies continue to shrink, and care must be taken to make sure they do not deplete all food stores. If it is warm enough for bees to take cleansing flights, it is likely warm enough to take a quick look in to check on food supplies. Always take into consideration windchill when peaking in. The bees taking cleansing flights are not affected by windchill as much as the cluster keeping the brood warm. Rapid heat loss will occur when removing the inner and outer covers.

Therefore make all checks as quick as possible. The colony movement is most likely occupying some of the upper box now if they have not moved up completely. If you are raising bees for honey or bees, you may want to add brood building patties toward the end of the month or the first of March. The queen will be fed more pollen, resulting in her laying more eggs. During sudden prolonged severe cold periods in February and March, colony mortality can be high if food is exhausted by the increasing population. Stay ahead of the colony increase and think about preswarm actions. Adding food to increase brood can stimulate large colony increases, and sudden prolonged warm periods will further add to their numbers. During extended periods of bad weather, the building colony can quickly deplete food stores. Keep checking the honey and sugar food supply!

By feeding pollen patties in February, you will increase the bee population. It will be very important to implement swarm prevention in March, April, and May. Always be aware of long periods of inclement weather that may occur after bees have begun the spring buildup. A beginner may not want to feed pollen patties their first year. Bee swarms reduce the remaining colony size. The beginner will end up with less bees instead of more bees.

The large and building population of bees can quickly consume large amounts of food if the weather is rainy and cold for a longer period. Food stores can be depleted very quickly. When stored food is depleted, the adult bees may cannibalize the larva and eggs. The colony may survive when this occurs, but the buildup will need to start over. Feeding may be the only way to help the bees through these cold and rainy periods. Planning ahead of time is critical.

March. Early March is the start of swarm prevention. This means that it is time for the first brood box rotation. Temperature and precipitation forecasts are very important in order to coordinate needed work with outside weather conditions and to anticipate the needs of the colony. This will likely require you to do your first rotations of brood boxes if the colony is now occupying the top brood box. On a warm day around fifty degrees, open the hive and look into the bottom brood box. Look for eggs or larva. The eggs and larva will normally be located on the uppermost part of the foundations in the bottom box if there are any. If you find eggs or larva in the bottom brood box, then do not rotate boxes. This will split the brood area and cause brood loss. Wait a week and recheck. Rotate the two brood boxes if no eggs or brood are found in the lower brood box. Just simply switch the top and bottom brood box positions.

There shouldn't be any supers on at this time. The queen will be laying at near capacity. Colony population can double in three weeks. Keep an eye on the trees and local plant growth. Trees will start to bud, providing pollen and dandelions will start growing. Look for trees and flowers that are getting ready to bloom. Honey supers are usually added in April, but an early warm-up may require you to add them early. Monitor the bee activity. The foragers start bringing in pollen on their sides and maybe some nectar in their honey stomach. The foragers will switch from all pollen to mostly all nectar when the main nectar flow starts. Every year may be slightly different, making it important to monitor both the bees and their nectar and pollen sources.

This is also a good time to start planning for colony splits if more colonies are wanted. Be informed about the weather forecasts, plant growth, and warming so that planning can be done to meet the needs of the bees. Trees and plants will start blooming. These are priorities for your bees. They will not miss the opportunity that the available nectar, pollen, warming weather, and longer days will provide for them to increase their numbers for swarming! When doing hive inspections, look for signs of diseases, such as spotty brood patterns, off-colored larva, or bad odors. A large number of dead bees can also indicate problems. The weaker, under fed colonies, with high-mite counts are usually the only bees that will experience these types of problems. The beginner beekeeper will not normally need to be concerned with diseases if they have taken care of their bees.

This is an important time to treat for mites. Most if not all mite treatments must be done prior to adding honey supers. Care must be taken to avoid contaminating the honey with chemicals. Therefore, early April will be the last chance to treat for mites until after the honey harvest in June or later.

April. Swarm prevention is becoming more important. A second brood box rotation as well as adding supers is a must. April is the month that bees swarm due to lack of space or because of a food shortage. Bees will swarm to reduce numbers in the hive, preventing the hive from starving. This month is very busy for both you and your bees. The increasing daylight hours, rainfall, and warm weather result in the start of the main nectar flow. The final brood box rotation should be done in early April and your first supers added at this time. The second brood box rotation is done exactly like the first one in March. Do not rotate if the bees are occupying both brood boxes. After rotating the brood boxes, add two supers for a large overwintered hive and one super for a new or smaller hive. Always add two supers when using the single brood box method. Add supers by the middle of April even if you could not rotate the boxes.

Do not add any supers if you are feeding the colony. Be aware of favorable weather and enough rain that keeps the flow going and the bees working. Predict swarming. A sudden long period of rain or cold will keep the bees in the hive. The cold and rain will not slow or stop the increasing number of bees in the hive. The new bees will be continually emerging from the capped brood. You will have to check to see if they gathered enough food before the rain so that they have enough food in the hive to prevent swarming. You may need to feed during this short period of bad weather.

Anticipate the need for food by checking the weather forecast for a prediction of rain or cold. Check the hive for swarm cells prior to this cold rainy weather. It is very important to remember that a large number of bees in the hive will consume a large amount of food stores in a short period of time. The population will also continue to build. If the bees run low on food, they will swarm. Adding supers in a timely manner is very important to keep your bees from swarming due to overcrowding and to keep your honey crop growing. Always keep an empty super on top. Add another super when the bottommost super has seven or eight frames of honey.

Most swarms in April are the day after an extended cold or rainy period usually occurring during the day's warm-up between 11:00 a.m. and 3:00 p.m. The hive will appear to have no activity on the outside on days that are rainy and cold. However, the interior will be full of working bees that are consuming food stores very rapidly. Even though the weather may not be favorable for swarming, the bees may swarm during cold and rainy weather. A colony does this when there is a very large population of bees with little food stores and no room to expand. They will swarm as a survival strategy. Swarms in early April are generally city swarms or beekeeper swarms, caused by over- or underfeeding. In our area, most wild swarms occur in mid-May. A swarm trap is a basic tool that all beekeepers need, especially beginners. Time to catch some free bees with a swarm trap. If your bees swarm, they could swarm again in eight to sixteen days. Keep checking for extra queen cells.

May. The month of May is the primary time for swarming in our area. April is the prime time for swarming due to food shortage or overcrowding due to early feeding. Swarming in May is primarily due to overcrowding, resulting from an abundant natural food supply. Stay ahead of your bees. Failure to prevent overcrowding will result in swarming. The colony has a natural instinct to reproduce by swarming. The bee population builds up before the main nectar flow starts. The main nectar flow is when many flowering plants are in bloom, providing an abundance of nectar.

The bees have a higher natural tendency to swarm during this period of abundance. The swarm will have the best chance of surviving and establishing a new colony. The remaining bees in the swarming colony that do not leave with the swarm also stand a better chance of surviving and rebuilding. There will be a large population of quality drones in May. Therefore this is a good time for queen rearing. Stay ahead of colony buildup by adding additional supers in a timely manner. Monitor for diseases, and keep a close eye on swarming possibilities.

Toward the end of May, the temperature will start to really warm up. This is the time to start thinking about hive ventilation. Hive ventilation is important in the warmer weather especially when the bees are trying to dry the honey down to about 18 percent before capping. The moisture from the evaporation process combined with the hot air in the hive will make it uncomfortable for the bees and will take the bees longer to reduce the moisture of the honey so that they can cap it. Adding a vent shim to the top of the hive is the easiest way. The hive top can be lifted slightly with 1/4 inch wood spacers to allow more airflow. A bigger space at the top can also make an easier entry for beetles. Place a screen over the hole in the inner cover to prevent beetles and other insects from entering when the top is raised.

June. Harvest the honey in the supers in June or early July. Colony population buildup will be slowing down due to the reduced nectar flow. Honey supers should be inspected for capping, and the harvest begins toward the end of the month. Harvest the capped honey only. The uncapped honey has too much moisture in it. This month can also be the start of robbing. The major nectar sources begin to disappear, and large numbers of scout bees will be looking for more sources of food. The smaller colonies and their food stores can and will become a target for the larger colonies. Entrance feeders and open feeding should be avoided as it will cause robbing. Make sure supers on colonies are not exposed for any amount of time when inspecting or harvesting.

Always clean up any wax comb or honey that has been dropped on or near the hive. Removed supers should be covered and protected until in the area where you are going to harvest the honey. This could be your kitchen or some other clean environment. Robbing behavior is much easier to prevent than it is to stop. A mite treatment should be done as soon as possible after the honey supers have been removed. A mite count will be done next month to check the effectiveness of the treatment.

Honey supers should be cleaned and stored. The bees can be allowed to clean the frames after harvesting. However, use caution as this can also start robbing. The frames with drawn out wax must be protected for use next year. Bees may still swarm during June, so keep an eye out for swarm cells during inspections. Supers may have to remain on the hive in years with continuing rainfall into July. The continued rainfall may keep the nectar flow going, resulting in too much honey being stored in the brood area. Always perform the required beekeeping tasks by observing the weather conditions and plant growth, not by the calendar.

You may see the bees hanging out on the front of the hive at night. This is normal. On hot and especially humid evenings, many bees will spend the night outside the hive, clinging to the front of the hive, or they may form a beard on the ground in front of the hive. This phenomenon is called *bearding*. The bees are trying to find a cooler place than the hot, humid hive. Consider adding a top venting shim to allow more airflow through the hive or a slotted bottom board to give the bees extra room at the bottom. The increased airflow will not only help cool the hive but it will also remove humidity. The bees will have an easier time removing excess moisture from the honey and will be able to cap it sooner. Bearding can also be a result of overcrowding in the hive. This can be corrected by adding a second brood box or temporarily adding a super.

Many beekeepers harvest their honey in late June or early July as the main (spring) honeyflow has ended. Decide if the fall weather is going to allow a good honeyflow. Consider allowing the bees to keep the fall flow to be stored as winter food. Honey is the best winter food for the bees. There will be less winter prep because the bees will more than likely have the food that they need for winter. After harvest, consider treating for mites. Use caution due to the temperature restrictions of most mite treatments. An improper treatment can result in the bees leaving (absconding). Always follow the manufacturer's instructions to avoid losing the bees and to avoid exposing yourself to the chemicals in the mite treatments.

In the months of July and August, the bees may seem to be foraging very heavily. This is usually the time of little or no nectar flow. The forager bees during these times may be collecting water instead of nectar. Water is used to cool the hive and for the other bees in the hive. The bees need lots of water. It is very important to provide the bees with a source of water.

July is robbing prevention, rapid mite growth, and the start of the hive beetles. Reduce entrances to the smallest opening that doesn't cause entrance congestion. If there are multiple hives, be aware not to let a strong hive rob a weak hive. Do not open up the hive for extended periods as other hives may try to rob the weaker hive after it is opened. Perform a mite count and treatment if needed. A treatment will be needed if the bees were not treated in June. Prepare for a rapid growth and spread of mites. This is commonly referred to as the mite bomb.

Increase hive ventilation and provide a water source if water is not available. When removing capped honey supers, make sure to clean up any spills and never leave wax comb removed during the inspection around any of the hives. Cleaned honey supers should be stored using a method that will protect the valuable frames of comb. Having drawn-out comb will provide your bees with a big start for next year. Energy expenditure is high for honeybees when it comes to drawing comb (4–9 lbs. of honey to produce 1 pound of beeswax).

Before harvesting the honey, make sure that there is honey in the brood area by checking the weight of the brood boxes. The bees will need food during the period of reduced or no nectar flow. You may need to feed some hives. Use caution when feeding if you have multiple hives due to robbing. Do not use feeding stimulates, such as Honey B Healthy at this time as it may cause robbing.

The goal is to reduce mite numbers and help the bees counteract effects of colony population decrease and mite population increase. This will be very important in the months of July, August, and September. Provide a source of water and some type or ventilation for hive cooling in hot weather. Feeders full of water (no syrup) can be used to make it easier for the bees to keep cool. This is especially important if the hives that are exposed to full sun. Add a vent shim or 1/4 spacers to lift the outer cover up slightly off the inner cover. You can also tip the outer cover to allow an air gap between the inner and outer covers. A screen should be placed over the inner cover hole when lifting the top to prevent easy access to the hive by unwanted insect like ants, wasps, or beetles.

However, no mite treatments can be used in a hive while supers are on. This could contaminate the honey with chemical residue. The period of little or no flowering plants for nectar is called dearth. The nectar dearth will become more prominent in August. Make sure that your bees have honey stored in the brood boxes. Do not remove honey from the brood area. It is not necessary to feed hives with ample food stores in the brood area at this time.

Hive beetles can become a problem if not controlled. Precautions for hive beetles should have already begun. Breaking the beetle life cycle is the best way to control the beetles. Oil traps or Swiffer pads can be placed into the hive to help get the beetles under control.

Always strive to be a responsible beekeeper. Not treating your hives will spread mites to any neighboring colonies. Become aware of any neighboring colonies. There could be wild colonies or another beekeeper's colonies. Both of these can be potential problems for you as well.

Splits

It is best to do most splits in May or June. The weather and available nectar will give the new colony enough food resources to help the new colony grow. April is a good time to split for swarm prevention. Making a split by removing the old queen is one of the best swarm control methods. Splitting a hive by removing the old queen will cause the old colony to become queenless. While the old hive makes a new queen, the hive will become broodless. No brood will make it easier to treat for mites. The bees will use this time to store more honey during the main nectar flow because they won't have to take care of any brood. Some large beekeepers use this method to increase the amount of honey that they will have to harvest. This also provides extra nucs to sell or to grow additional hives.

Large colonies that are building very fast can be used for making increase and splits by removing a frame or two of brood and making nucs.

Help Save the Bees

Helping

Anyone can help the bees by providing a safe source of water in the hot dry summer and by planting flowers that bloom July through September. Many who want to help the bees plant flowers that bloom in April through early June, and the bees never come. The reason that they don't come is because flowers that bloom at this time are competing with the many wild flowers. Food is plentiful at this time. Scout bees find the best source of food (nectar and pollen) and go back and give great detail to the foragers where to go. The scout bees perform a waggle dance in the hive to share the exact location of the best food source. So to best help the bees, plant flowers or shrubs that bloom from the end of June through September. This is a time that the bees are in need of food and a water source because it is dry and most of the wild flowers are not blooming at this time.

There are many sources for flowers to plant on the internet including the Indiana DNR site (in.gov/dnr/entomolo/files/ep-Gardening_for_Honey_Bees.pdf). Providing a water source, such as a fountain or a bird bath, will be a great way to help the bees to safely obtain the water that they need. The water source that is provided should have a way that the bees can safely get to the water without drowning. This can be accomplished by adding rocks or objects that the bees can land on. Wood pieces or chips will float on the water, providing another great way. Azolla plants can be used in a container pond or fountain. The water doesn't have to be perfectly clean. The bees will be happy that you are helping them.

This is an excellent time to get close to the bees and become more comfortable around them. Also you can allow the bees to clean the honey super frames after harvesting the honey. The water source and honey must be a distance from any hive to prevent robbing or to prevent getting near bees that are defending their hive. Many forager bees will come to get the water and honey. These bees don't have to protect their hive. They are only interested in getting food and water. Therefore they have no reason to sting you unless you smash them or you attempt to touch them. You can put water and honey on your hands and fingers. The bees will land on you to get the water and honey without stinging.

There is always a possibility of getting stung, but this is a very, very low or no possibility. Avoid wearing smelly perfumes or hair sprays. These are foragers, so you may not want them to go into your hair or land on you where you don't want them to land. More than likely, they won't bother you at all. This is just a precaution. This is an excellent opportunity to take pictures of you with the bees. Show the pictures to your friends. They may think that you are crazy, but you will know that you had little chance of getting stung.

The information in this book is intended to help the new beekeeper succeed in their first year. There are many ways to do things successfully. Suggestions have been made as a better practice for the beginner. My goal has always been to help new beekeepers and to reduce the cost of beekeeping. The tools and supplies that I have recommended are intended to limit your initial cost while making sure you have the things that you need. Most all the beekeeping tools and supplies are imported from China.

So don't think that buying from the big companies gets you a better product or an American product. Shop around for the best price. Keep your cost low so that beekeeping will be fun and not an expensive hobby. Don't limit yourself to the recommendations in this book or any other source. Use your imagination. A big part of the beekeeping experience is to build, research, learn, and experiment. You can think about how to do things different or better once you become familiar and know how to take care of bees. Have fun!

Glossary

Apiary. An apiary is the area where the beehives are located.

Apiculture. Apiculture is the study of beekeeping.

Bearding. This describes the behavior of the bees forming on the outside of the hive on a hot and humid day. This usually occurs later in the day. Many bees hang out outside because it is hot and humid in the inside.

Bee escape. A bee escape or a bee escape board is used to allow the bees to leave the honey super and not be able to return. This is used when harvesting the honey from the supers.

Bee cycle. The yearly long cycle where the bees carry out their basic needs to collect food and water, raise their young, and reproduce by casting off new swarms.

Beetles. A very small black bug that enters the hive to lay their eggs and consume food. If left uncontrolled will cause the colony to move elsewhere.

Beetle life cycle. Beetles lay their eggs in the hive on the foundations. The eggs hatch into larva and feed on the honey. They exit out of the hive and enter the ground to become beetles. They then return as adult beetles.

Bottom board. The bottom board is the lowest part of the hive. It supports the hive boxes and provide the entrance to the hive.

Brace and burr comb. Brace comb is comb built between frames. It is used to support or brace the frames or comb. Burr comb is the wax on top of the frames. It is a filler-type comb.

Brood area. The brood area on the comb where the queen lays her eggs.

Brood box. This is the deep hive box that holds the frames where the queen lays eggs and the bees are raised for eggs to becoming a bee.

Candy board or shim. A candy board is a means of providing food for the winter. A candy board is used by placing a sugar mixture or dry sugar into a small shim and placed into the hive above the uppermost brood box.

Closer board. This board slides in the screened bottom board. It is used to close the screened opening for winter.

Cluster. This refers to the sphere-shaped area where the bees stay in and raise their young in the cold winter months. The outside of the cluster is formed by a layer of bees facing inward. This insulates the center area of the cluster where the temperature remains in the nineties even when very cold outside.

Colony. The colony refers to the actual bee population in the hive.

Colony health. This is when the bees are strong and free of disease. Adequate food supplies and feeding at the correct time plays an important part of colony health.

Commercial beekeepers. Are large beekeepers who raise bees to pollinate crops and/or raise bees for honey. Large for profit beekeepers.

Debris board. This is the same as closer board.

Deep. A deep is also referred to as a brood box. It is the largest hive body where the queen lays her eggs and the eggs become bees.

Drone. The drone is the male bee. It is a large bee with a rounded body. Drones can't sting because they don't have a stinger.

Entrance reducer. An entrance reducer is a piece of wood with two sizes of hole. It is placed between the bottom board and the first deep box. It serves as the hive entrance, and the opening size can be increased or decreased to allow the bees to better protect their hive from insects like wasps, beetles, and other neighboring colonies.

Fall flow. Fall flow is when the many flowers bloom in the fall. This is when nectar will again become available for the bees. This is also the last chance for the bees to store food for the winter.

Feeder box. This is a term used to describe a honey super that the bees are allowed to keep year round. This is mainly used on a one-brood box method. Honey is never taken from this box.

Feeder entrance. This type of feeder is placed in the front entrance. The entrance reducer will have to cut off to make room for this feeder. This is an easy feeder to use if only one or two hives. Caution must be used to prevent robbing if there are multiple hives in the area. Avoid using feeding stimulates if there is more than one hive.

Feeder frame. This is a plastic container the size of a frame. One frame is removed, and the frame feeder takes its place. Sugar water is used as food. Use extreme care due to the easy possibility of drowning.

Feeder hive top. This type of feeder is placed on top of the inner cover. A spare box will be used to in close this feeder. There are several types of hive top feeders. There are round, rectangular, and jar hive top-type feeders. These are also easy to use.

Foundation. This is the sort of flat surface on which the bees make the wax comb.

Frame. The frame is the structure that holds the foundation.

Frame rest. A frame rest is a metal frame that is temporarily placed on the hive. It is used to hold the frames removed during hive inspections. This prevents the frames and foundations from being damaged during the inspections.

Harvest. This is the uncapping and spinning the honey out of honey super foundations. The honey will be poured through a screen to remove wax pieces making it ready to consume.

Hive. This is the actual wooden physical structure where the bees will be residing.

Hive management. This is the yearlong anticipation of the needs of the honeybees. The beekeeper must understand where the bees are in their yearly bee cycle and the weather conditions affecting them.

Hive tool. This is a tool designed to safely remove frames from the hive and to also separate the hive boxes.

Honeyflow. The honeyflow is when there are flowers or trees blooming providing nectar for the bees to make honey.

Inner cover. The inner cover is an almost flat piece of wood covering the top most hive box. This cover is used to prevent the bees from gluing the outer cover on while maintaining the 3/8 bee space.

Intruders. Any insect or animal that enters the hive to steal honey. These include ants, wasps, beetles, and mice.

Langstroth hive. It is a hive with removable parts. It was invented in 1852 by L. L. Langstroth and is still used by most beekeepers in the United States today.

Medium. It is the midsize hive box. It is normally used for honey storage being taken off the hive for human consumption.

Moisture board. This is a board placed on top of the hive in the winter to absorb moisture. It prevents the moisture from dripping on the bees.

Mouse guards. Is a metal piece with small holes that prevents mice from entering the hive in the winter. The bees can come and go on warm days.

Nucleolus hive (nuc). A nuc is a small five-frame hive box. It is used for starting a colony or for a smaller colony.

Oil pan. An oil pan is placed in the grove under the screened bottom board. It is used to catch beetle larva and mites that fall out of the hive.

Outer cover. This cover protects the hive from the weather, such as rain and snow.

Pest management. This is controlling the insects and animals that will damage the colony.

Pheromone. This is the sent that the bees use to signal other bees. The queen pheromone directs the organization of the worker bees. The guard bees give off an alarm pheromone to notify all the bees in the hive of danger.

Pollen patties. Protein-based food for the bees. There are two types: brood and winter pollen patties. Brood patties are 40 or more percent pollen and are used to stimulate the queen to lay eggs in early spring or late summer. Winter patties are around 4 percent protein. They are used to provide extra protein for winter food.

Pollen substitutes. These are other sources of protein other than the normal source of protein for the bees. The normal sources for bees are flower and tree pollen.

Requeen. Requeening means to replace the queen in the hive. This is done to replace a queen that is old or is not laying as she should. Requeening is also used to change the traits of the colony, such as aggressive behavior.

Queen. The queen is the largest female in the hive. She lays the eggs and emit a pheromone that keeps the hive working.

Queen excluder. The queen excluder is a slatted covering that is designed so that the larger queen cannot get through, but the smaller worker bees can. It is made of metal or plastic.

Robbing. Robbing is when stronger hive steals the honey of the weaker colony. This usually results in the queen and the entire colony being killed by the stronger colony.

Scout bees. Scout bees are forager bees who go out in search for food. They also search for a new home for a swarm. The scout bees tell the other bees exactly where the best food sources are.

Screened bottom board. This is a bottom board with a screen which is designed to allow mites to fall out of the hive.

Shallow. A shallow box is also called a honey super. It is the smallest of the hive boxes at 5 3/4 inches deep.

Slatted bottom board. The slatted bottom board is originally designed for a solid bottom board to increase airflow. It is now also used as a spacer on a screened bottom board making the lower part of the frames in the bottom brood box more appealing to the queen.

Smoker. A smoker is the device where material are ignited to allow smoke to be delivered to the hive when working with the hive. Smoke blocks the alarm pheromone of the guard bees.

Stands. Any type of blocks, wood, or anything designed to safely hold the hive off the ground.

Super(s). This is another name for a medium or shallow hive box. This is where the bees store honey that is going to harvested for human consumption.

Swarm box. A swarm box is used to attract and catch a swarm that has left a hive.

Swarms, swarming. This is the reproduction means of the honeybee. When the hive swarms, up to 2/3 of the bees leave the original hive along with the old queen. The exiting bees go out to find a new home. The old hive will have a new queen in the making. Swarming is easily identified by the number of bees in the air. The bees will be flying high and low in a large area. They will eventually form an oval ball on a nearby tree or structure.

Tanging. Tanging is making a loud ringing or clanging sound. Pots and metal objects are banged together to cause bee swarms to settle near the ground.

Varroa mites. The Varroa is a tiny mite that attaches itself to the bee and causes disease and deformity to the bee.

Varroa Varro. Is a mite that causes damage and spreads diseases to the bees.

Vent shim. A vent shim is a small box usually less than three inches. The box has small holes with screens to allow airflow. This box is placed on top of the inner cover.

Wax cap. A wax cap is a thin layer of wax that is used by the bees to seal their honey in the comb.

Winter preparation. Winter preparation means preparing the hive for winter, controlling mites and moisture, and insuring that the bees have an adequate food stores for the winter.

Worker bees. Worker bees are all females. They do all the work in and out of the hive.

About the Author

· ·

Earl Schnell is a beekeeper of more than five years. He started a local beekeeping supply store and started a local beekeeping club. He wants to help beekeepers reduce or eliminate mistakes, saving both time and money. He has a desire to help every beekeeper to become successful in their first year and beyond. He understands the many problems that the beginning beekeepers will have to overcome. He hopes to continue doing everything possible to make beekeeping fun while educating the public about the importance of honeybees. Earl hopes to someday have a property with a building dedicated to helping beekeepers and the public of all ages to learn about and experience honeybees up close. He would love to hear from anyone who can help.

CPSIA information can be obtained
at www.ICGtesting.com
Printed in the USA
LVHW071539280122
709674LV00024B/2481

9 781662 466540